THE MUSICAL FACULTY

THE MUSICAL FACULTY

ITS ORIGINS AND PROCESSES

WILLIAM WALLACE

GYAN

Published by

Gyan Publishing House
5, Ansari Road
Daryaganj, New Delhi-110002
Phone: 011-47034999, 9811692060
E-mail: books@gyanbooks.com

Distribution Network
gyanbooks.com
India, USA, Canada, UK, Australia

ISBN: 978-93-7225-206-4 (PB)

First Published, 1914

2nd Impression 2026

Printed at: Gyan Press, Delhi.

THE MUSICAL FACULTY
Author: WILLIAM WALLACE

THE MUSICAL FACULTY

THE MUSICAL FACULTY

ITS ORIGINS AND PROCESSES

BY

WILLIAM WALLACE

AUTHOR OF "THE THRESHOLD OF MUSIC"

MACMILLAN AND CO., LIMITED
ST. MARTIN'S STREET, LONDON

1914

PREFACE

THIS book deals with the mechanism of the musical sense more closely than was possible or expedient in its predecessor, *The Threshold of Music*. Its aim is psychological rather than musical, and it records in outline the mental processes concerned with the creation and production of Music.

It has been my endeavour to avoid repetition, and in returning to the question of Heredity, I have been influenced by the fact that since *The Threshold* was published, some attention has been given to "Music" by those who are applying Mendel's Law to Man. What follows on this subject should be read along with the chapter on Heredity and Environment in my former book.

The text is not burdened with references to works on Psychology, for the reason that Music, when discussed at all, even in the larger treatises, has been considered almost entirely from the outside.

The psychologist perhaps will join issue with me for disregarding a terminology which has not yet been standardized, but I trust I am not to be deemed blameworthy in using everyday expressions for ordinary occurrences.

I have kept in view the dual nature of the work, and while writing primarily for scientific men, I have not lost sight of the necessity for simplicity in discussing its purely musical aspects. At the same time I believe that musicians will find interesting the analysis of mental acts which they themselves perform in their daily vocation.

Long personal experience in the Art itself, and practical study in the Profession which is concerned with the functions of the Brain, alone have guided me in my investigations.

Therefore, while disclaiming any title to dogmatize, I venture, not without diffidence, to put forward these results of observation and research in the hope that they may suggest a field for wider and more minute inquiry.

My last word here must be that when my earlier training forced me to rely upon the evidence of my senses, the realities of life became insistent beyond all conception of poignancy, and it was only by taking refuge in the infinities of Music that I found the means for reconciling these realities with dreams.

WILLIAM WALLACE.

LONDON, *July*, 1914.

CONTENTS

Soe there bee these Ladders, the Scala Tympani and the Scala Vestibuli, leading Man knoweth not whither. For whether of the one or of the other the End bee Musick, this is sure, that noe Man climbeth a Ladder bee it not set firm, and hee that gaineth the topmost Heighth doth view a Prospect of great Pleasure to the Eie, and, if Birdes doe sing, of Comfort to the Eare. And truly it was said of Jacob's Ladder, which is to bee found in Holy Writ, that there were Angels ascending it, and using it in wholesome Manner. Therefore if the Angels did use it for the Purpose of climbing into Heaven, wee Mortals, in our Sadness, would be ill-favoured to put aside such glad Machinery, and vie with those whose welcome Assurancies lie in our travelling the same Path as they.

Multum laboravi ut hæc ossicula cum membrana timpani in situ naturaliter delinearentur, sed pene impossibile est : quorum tamen descriptio mihi videtur potius confusionem quam scientiam paritura.

Verheyen : *Anat. Hum. Corp.* Lib. 1.
apud Coloniæ : MDCCXIII.

CHAPTER I

GENERAL PRINCIPLES

It is not difficult to understand the reluctance of scientific investigators to indulge in theories connected with the brain which are not supported by rigidly authenticated evidence. No state of knowledge can be anticipated which furnishes a key to the complicated processes of the mind. Scientific research, however, has opened up the vast field of the functions of the brain, and while there are innumerable points of minute detail yet to be settled, along with others which are bound to arise, the broad facts concerning the sensory and motor functions are not in dispute.

We need not discuss whether these functions are localized in definite areas, or are inherent in groups of cells closely related to one another : it must, however, be emphasized at the outset that no grounds exist for identifying the manifold operations of the mind with special cerebral tracts. In other words, the higher brain centres concerned with the will, the emotions, and all the varieties of creative activity, are not as yet capable of definite localization.

At the same time, we may quite reasonably desire that those mental processes which are not primarily to be assigned to sensory or motor centres should be classed under one term to describe them and convey a clear meaning as to the operations with which they are concerned. For although all ultimately are referable to some group of these centres by minute analysis, we are still at a loss for a word—a "short title," in fact—to describe the impulses of the mind which belong properly to the creative faculty, and which arise without apparent external stimulus. Bastian[1] suggested "Perceptive Centres," but these cannot be isolated from the sensori-motor tract.

It cannot be denied that the word "Psychology" is somewhat out of favour, for although at its birth it conveyed a definite meaning and had a limited application, it has come to be the pass-word for a great many crude ideas which may have kinship with the ψυχή, but are singularly lacking in the λόγος. Its affinities, "psychism" and "psychic," are too often bandied about in an atmosphere tainted with more than a suspicion of charlatanism, and are designedly used to impress with some cryptic meaning the plain person in the presence of one who poses

[1] Bastian: *The Brain as an Organ of the Mind*, Lond. 1885, p. 525.

as being "in touch with the infinite." Unfortunately the province of the scientific inquirer has been invaded by a horde of loose thinkers and self-centred egoists, who persuade themselves that they have some secret power not bestowed upon ordinary mortals.

In science the conscientious student again and again finds himself forestalled in terminology by some inexpert investigator, who has laid hands upon and vulgarized a word which by no means can be twisted to describe his theories or presumed discoveries. Thus the fitting word "Phrenology" was appropriated by Gall and Spurzheim and applied to an assumption of which there is this to be said that it contains neither *φρήν* nor *λόγος*. It is not a little singular that, valuable and permanent as were their studies of the spinal cord, they learnt so little from their investigations (for what has been demonstrated must form the text-book for further research), that they imperilled their reputation as accurate observers by advancing wild and wholly unscientific theories when they travelled up to the calvarium.

The old anatomists were wise in their generation in giving either their own or fanciful names to special structures when they found themselves at a loss for definite terms, but modern methods demand a terminology which conveys an accurate localization of the part to which the old name was given. Still, after all, theirs was merely the anticipation of our own methods, for when a new world is created, such as the domain of electricity, there is nothing for it but to invent symbols and ideographs to replace highly complex phraseology. Hence, Ohm, Volta, Ampère, Watt, Joule, and Kelvin, who in their life-time stood for human energy, now stand for energy in physical shape,—short words and to the point.

There is nothing more significant of the newness of Music than the fact that when we wish to discuss it on broad grounds and apart from its elemental, its skeletal structure, we are compelled to borrow terms which specially belong to other arts, while these arts have adopted musical expressions which are not always appropriate.

Possibly we must wait for the coming of some psychologist who will devote his attention, less to a study of the purely elementary sensory and motor functions which he himself can perform, than to the investigation of the mental construction of the man who creates a work of art. From the meagre amount of space devoted to Music in works specially dealing with Psychology, we gather that their writers leave the subject alone because they are not able to draw upon their own experience in discussing it. What we are told about Music partakes mainly of a writer's personal views as to the æsthetic value of works whose merits were never in question.

Music as an art is cursed by the grievous fact that

at every stage, where the emotional significance alone ought to count, some analyst intrudes and dwells lovingly upon technicalities, with all the jargon of the text-book, and evades the clear thought that leapt untrammelled from the composer's mind. The amazing thing is that Music goes on in spite of these dissections. The drag upon its ceaselessly revolving wheel has been the deadweight of grammar. Music is primarily and always an ear-sense, and the fittest that survive are those who have been moved by what they heard, not by what they saw of the written notes. There is a continual struggle between emotion and grammar; every step in musical history demonstrates that emotion and intuition led the way, while grammar, driven to preserve its self-respect, followed when it had mustered assurance enough, and had no scruples about abandoning entirely its own teachings so as to make a show of being with the vanguard.

Those who have impressed themselves most deeply upon the records of Music have been men who heard for themselves, and trusted to their instinct rather than to a prescribed rule.

Doubtless the acquired technique of the art was beneficial to many, and its artifices were useful in spinning out a tenuous idea so as to magnify it into bombast. It would be a dreary prospect were every act and thought of man to be reduced to a statistical diagram, and it is difficult to see where our

English literature would be were the plain statement of personal experience to be rejected because, let us say, of a split infinitive. Music is a spontaneous act of creation, and it only matters when it asserts itself so strongly as to reflect a free and individual impression without the mechanical aid of instruction. It is in this that a study of the musical faculty presents difficulties. The gift may be inherent and spontaneous : it may be an acquisition deliberately cultivated to such a point as to pass for genuine creative ability. Thus there are two clearly defined processes, each of which has its own distinctive features. On the one hand, we have the very matrix and essence of sound dominated by physical laws ; on the other, this form of sound can be converted into a fluid medium of thought, unconcerned with, but at the same time unconsciously obedient to, these laws. Thus it is possible to produce a musical work by two different and apparently irreconcilable efforts.

Let us take examples. A boy of twelve, let us say, has had no musical instruction beyond some lessons at the piano which teach him the notation, but he undergoes a subjective education as well when he hears members of his family play and sing, and when he is taken to concerts. He wishes to amuse himself by "writing something," and produces the awkward and angular affair that we should expect, founded upon and echoing the music that he has been taught.

But in its midst we find a progression or modulation, a line of melody or a harmony whose origin cannot be traced to anything which he has played or heard. We ask, then, how he chanced by ear to discover a correct though unusual arrangement of sounds, and wrote it down because it pleased him.

Again, let us consider the case of a man who has reached the age of 25 without showing any natural musical gift. He has a great love for music and a wide knowledge of the classics, but no keenly sensitive ear. By close application to the groundwork of the art he masters the principles of counterpoint, fugue, and construction, and by dint of intelligence, perseverance, and taste makes something that is not unlike hundreds of other compositions.

As far as Music as a medium of thought is concerned he is working out on paper a mechanical problem in which the eye is used more than the ear, and at best he deals with musical platitudes in sentences and phrases which any one with the musical sense can complete after having heard only a bar or two.

The relation between the eye and the ear which will be considered later on, has not, in this case, reached an advanced stage of development. It may, indeed, be questioned whether the ear, or music-sense, contributes much to the result, which is obtained by the eye-study of music-diagrams. The laws of construction in a fugue, for instance, have been so clearly defined that this form of composition can be produced very much in the way that the schoolboy writes Latin verses, using all the threadbare clichés of the classics. No one would dream of regarding the boy as a poet, no matter how closely he came near the Augustan models, and similarly the correctness of a machine-made fugue would not entitle its builder to a place among those whose music-sense was finding an outlet for sounds that were heard as sounds and not as symbols on paper.

It is obvious that in these two examples we have two distinct mental processes at work. They illustrate one of the perplexities that are met with in an analysis of the creative faculty in Music. In every art there is much that is accidental: the painter, dipping his brush into the wrong colour, may put on his canvas a smudge which suggests to him the conversion of an unsatisfactory picture into an enduring joy. The sculptor's sketch in clay may slip overnight into a shape that ends the difficulties of weeks past. The composer, testing his work at the piano, strikes a wrong note or chord which leads him into the tide of sound that many a time had escaped him.

It is impossible to ignore instances such as these, even although they do not fall properly within our study, for the reason that the intellect and the will have not a part in their production. They are on the same basis as many discoveries in science which did not arise from a logical deduction, but from a breakdown of the apparatus in the laboratory.

In Music, no matter what the result may be, we have a vast number of minds of widely different calibres engaged in its production. It has been the case, more frequently in the past than in the present, that the creative gift has been found in the minds of many who, according to modern standards, were illiterate. This doubtless was due to scanty educational methods as well as to social and economic conditions which may throw some light upon our inquiry.

The subject is not one which can be narrowed down to one explicit issue, and this may account, to some degree, for the reluctance of the professed psychologist to handle it. A glance at Helmholtz,[1] Stumpf,[2] or Gurney,[3] to mention only three formidable treatises, may well discourage the student. But in a question of this kind, experience, whether individual in its nature or proved in the case of others, may, with all its mistakes and misconceptions, be of more avail than reams of theory.

[1] Helmholtz: *On the Sensations of Tone*, translated by A. J. Ellis, 3rd edition, Lond. 1895.

[2] Stumpf: *Tonpsychologie*, erster Band, 1883, zweiter Band, 1890, Leipzig.

[3] Gurney: *The Power of Sound* Lond. 1880.

While, therefore, much that follows may seem at first to have only a remote connection with the problem, we cannot afford to pass over anything that helps us to a fuller understanding of an absorbing, and at the same time an extremely complicated study.

CHAPTER II

A READJUSTMENT OF VALUES

In analyzing the musical faculty we are confronted with the difficulty of eliminating many processes and considering one only as a separate and self-contained whole.

There is no mental or physical act in Music that stands absolutely alone. All are linked up in a nexus so complicated that it is impossible to follow one thread without taking account of the minute strands that find their way into it, often so unexpectedly, from other parts of the web.

This overlapping occurs frequently at places where the line of thought has appeared to run untrammelled and free. But in the loom of the mind, while the warp is tense, there are many shuttles, and in the texture to be woven these play in and out to form intricate shapes and variegated patterns. In order to display the fabric we must ever be anticipating parts of the design that have yet to be unfolded ; we must constantly be looking back to sections, some fringe of which is essential to the larger plan.

The lustrous garment of Music in which we enwrap our minds in these days may appear too opulent, too garish for an art that was well content with the "white samite" of an earlier time; but in whatever period the web was warped, of whatever threads the habiliments were wrought, the best that every age gave forth seemed to it as cloth of gold, for man could make no better,—he could weave no better than what the experience of his own time had to teach.

Every period of Music has had its wonders, each more startling than the last, but this is an age of grey matter, and it is with grey matter that we are here concerned.

The speculative discussion of Music demands at the outset the recognition of clearly defined limitations, namely, the absence of any standard of excellence. In the other arts human experience has discovered what is best, not by any method of dogmatism, but by a gradual process of selection spread out over centuries, and this has been found to harmonize with the development of man's æsthetical judgment. Again and again a School has arisen in Painting or in Architecture to play havoc with the cherished ideals of some predecessor. The strife has been interminable and will never end, though, as time goes on, and as each party can look back upon hosts of precedents, it will reduce itself to the level of a Kriegspiel.

It is doubtful if any great new School in the other arts will ever arise, for it will need to be so overwhelmingly powerful as to compel man to readjust his perceptions and to submit his thought to revolutionary changes. It is impossible to conceive how the sculptor or painter can make any abrupt departure from well-established conventions, for what he has to express is concrete and his theme remains unalterable, no matter how far he may carry his idealism. He is hampered at every turn by tradition : all that he can do is to work according to the old formulæ, bringing to bear upon them the spirit of the age in which he lives. Time is his most formidable rival, and every bygone period of art confronts him, surveying his efforts with gentle irony.

His limitations are even further restricted. He may give unchecked rein to his imagination, but everything that he expresses, if it is to convince others and to stimulate their minds so as to accord with his own, must convey something not too remote for their comprehension. He may invent, but the invention must to a large extent agree with the experience of others. He may take liberties with the conventions of technique, but the sculptor cannot make man other than in his own image, and however distorted the eye of the landscape-painter may be, even in his wildest riot of paint he cannot change the face of nature.[1]

In Music the limitation referred to—the absence of any standard of excellence—is not to be regretted. It is all to the advantage of the composer. He has no traditions to fetter him: he has no "Old Masters" to refer to: the formulæ which he employs are of his own creation. Whether his work is good or bad is not a question definitely to be settled in his own day. Proceedings in Music which were anathematized twenty—nay, ten—years ago are now recognized and admitted within the pale; melodic progressions which, not so long ago, sounded anarchistic, are to-day *plus royalistes que le Roy*.

The musical faculty is ever undergoing changes, and those who create and those who listen to Music are conscious that they too are changing, bringing to birth or appreciating sounds which at one time would have been detestable to them. We cannot account for these changes unless we assume that the musical faculty, unlike those involved in other arts, is in a

[1] It would be affectation to disregard any new movement in the fine arts, however extravagantly it chose to express itself. Those who class themselves under some "istic" heading, or under no heading at all, either are convinced that the pictures are true records of what they have seen, or they are poseurs. In both cases there is a mental factor which has already engaged the attention of the alienist.

state of evolution, and while it must be admitted that to prove a negative is difficult, particularly as regards a mental phase, no argument so far has been advanced to invalidate the assumption. At the same time it cannot be denied that, whatever the merits of the theory, a close study of the history of the art shows that the musical faculty of the composer of to-day is very different from that of the composer of a century ago. I am not concerned with the *æsthetical* results: let that be made perfectly clear. Every composition of ambitious character gives a clue, by internal evidence, to the degree of sensitiveness of the composer's psychico-auditory system, but it is irrelevant to drag in æsthetical questions which are not at issue. Let us discriminate. Every music-lover has his enthusiasms: no one would wish to tamper with them. But in this investigation we have not to throw light upon existing works of art, but to study the condition of brain that had to exist before the production of any kind of Music, whether good or bad, was possible.

For a clear understanding of all questions relating to the conception of Music we ought to rely upon the composer, but it seldom happens that he has had the opportunity for investigating such problems. On the other hand, in the case of lay writers—writers who have not the creative faculty in Music—we find almost without exception one flaw which vitiates their argument. We find in fact that they are lovers of

Music with special preferences, if not strong prejudices.

Let me give two instances. In a book published in 1874,[1] the year in which Verdi's *Requiem* was produced, and two years before the first performance of Wagner's *Ring*, the author confesses that at one time he was "decidedly prejudiced" against the Music of the Future; but he goes on to say that "after patient study of these [Wagner's] operas I became so susceptible of their higher dramatic beauties that I lost much of my relish for the older Italian opera, which began to appear highly unnatural." He adds that others underwent a similar experience. This account of his own personal development gives us important testimony regarding his musical appreciation. In his case, indeed, training and cultivation caused his musical centres to respond to a stimulus which at first was ineffective. This is the kind of evidence that is valuable.

Again, in a book published in 1880,[2] the author challenged, with four large pages of musical quotation, Wagner's method of recitative in *Lohengrin*, and took exception to a procedure which at that date had been in vogue for more than thirty years. At the same time, from the clues which he gave to his pre-

[1] Sully: *Sensation and Intuition: Studies in Psychology and Æsthetics*, Lond. 1874, p. 242, *n*.

[2] Gurney: *The Power of Sound*, Lond. 1880, p. 502.

ferences in music, we are led to infer that he was not in sympathy with the latest development of the art in his own day, and this kind of evidence also is valuable.

Thus from the works of two deep thinkers, writing within six years of one another about philosophical matters in Music, we have separate points of view which cannot be reconciled.

The bearing of this is important, for many writers upon whom we have relied for a reasoned exposition of Music, have shown that while they have gone to history for their references, they have not gone to history for their proofs. They have accepted all Music as having a fixed base, while history demonstrates that its centre of gravity is constantly being shifted, not by popular opinion, but by the evolution of the art itself, by those fluctuations of thought which have specially affected it. They have accepted it as a personal mental stimulus, and have not taken into account a host of conditions appertaining to the period, the special teaching of the moment, the condition of public taste, and the development of the musical faculty.

Many loose comparisons and analogies have resulted from this. Sometimes, for instance, it is asserted that Beethoven is in Music what Pheidias was in Sculpture. This is a sweeping comparison, based upon the assumption that no composer greater than Beethoven will ever arise, and as far as history goes it cannot be supported. We know, in fact, that Pheidias was the culminating point of the renaissance of an art which had been wiped out in the Persian wars, and had to begin afresh. This art, further, was two, three, perhaps even four thousand years old at the time when Pheidias flourished, while, above all, the world has had nearly two thousand five hundred years since his day to make up its mind as to the merits of his work. Its value to us is as historical as it is æsthetical.

But again, Beethoven was the culminating point of an art that was in his day barely a century old. Harmony had only come into existence in the previous five hundred years; there was, besides, no renascence or renaissance, for at no time had a great period of Music been dead and forgotten, waiting for the god who was to fan the ashes.

It would be rash, with less than a century in which to make up our minds, and with musical thought in a perpetual state of fluidity and transition, to assert that Beethoven will never be excelled. What he is to-day in the minds of many does not affect the point. Generous impulse and emotion are not the most trustworthy guides in a study of this kind, and they cannot make a Beethoven into a Pheidias at will.

Those who have traced for themselves the various

periods of Music will not dispute the fact that if we regard Music for the moment as a record of the human brain and detach it from all æsthetical relations, we are in a position to study its development almost as it were under the microscope, scrutinizing it as we might the growth of an organism from generation to generation, and noting the appearance of some character designed to meet the conditions of a new environment.

To whatever school of biology we pin our faith, we find in Music the results of a phase of evolution which doubtless in time to come will be considered along with the other evidences of intellectual activity. The biologist pursues his researches among forms of life which by immense rapidity of reproduction supply him in a brief space of time with families and generations whose constants and variations he can compare minutely. The most recent studies in chemistry have demonstrated that a body may undergo changes so rapidly that there is scarcely time in which to apply a test.[1]

Music, however, while its later progress has been

[1] "Niton, an emanation of Radium, disintegrates and half of it has changed into Radium A in about four days. In three minutes Radium A has half changed into Radium B, which changes into Radium C in 27 minutes. Radium C′ has a half-life of 19·5 minutes: Radium C″ is half-gone in 2·5 minutes, forming Radium D." Sir William Ramsay: Presidential Address at the British Association, 1911.

swift, has moved with sufficient deliberation to give us time to study its various stages, and by reconstructing its life-history we can make a diagram to illustrate the advance made in a very gradual progress spread over centuries. But infinitesimal as that growth was when noted from one period to another, and rapid as it has been in our own time, it shows material contrasts which justify our conclusions.

We find that a particular school of composition presents characters so definite that the student can identify it, just as a naturalist refers a living entity to its genus or natural order. It is evident that what may be called the "minute anatomy" of Music shows an organization which can be recognized and classified. It would be beyond human powers to indicate the exact moment when a variation in technique or construction made its appearance,—a modification of slight account when it was made, but destined to carry development a stage further. The historian and archæologist have already done much to simplify the task of making deductions from the data supplied by different periods. The difficulties that we have to encounter do not belong to the subject itself, but arise from the mental attitude of not a few musicians who are unable to discriminate between the æsthetical value of a composition and the light that it throws upon the composer's musical faculty.

It is no unusual thing for a theory to be challenged

by those who would be disturbed in their peace of mind were it to gain even a limited acceptance. In Music it is the case that the preferences and more especially the dislikes of individuals assert themselves with a violence that is rarely to be met with outside theology.

There are Mendels in biology and Mendelssohns in Music, and to suggest that the *Elijah*, for example, may be typical of a taste that some now regard as obsolete and of a generation that has drawn its last gasp, may be a thousand times more heretical, nay, criminal, than to cast doubts upon the "potency" of the Mendelian formula because at present it has only a restricted application. Mendelssohn, however, or any other composer, represents to the scientific inquirer merely a type of mind that was concerned with the development of Music, and his work is to be investigated for scientific purposes solely in comparison with antecedent and subsequent phases of the art. The student who pursues his researches scientifically cannot afford to deal in large assumptions; therefore it is idle to quarrel with a theory because we do not understand it, or to resort to mediæval casuistry because we do not agree with it.

When a musician asserts that the so-called incoherency of the ultra-modern style of composition is a sign of degeneracy, he is making a statement more pregnant, perhaps, than he suspects. But when, instead of adducing analogies from history and proofs in support of his argument, he proceeds to demolish it by wild and contradictory rhetoric, he scarcely convinces us of his authority to speak. We need not lose patience with the host of writers upon Music who establish theories upon the ground of personal bias. Many æsthetical questions must be left for a later generation to decide, and it is simpler to accept them now than to assail them. But beyond them there is another which can be immediately discussed in the impartial spirit of inquiry.

If we study musical history, we find it established almost as a law that one large and spacious period was followed by a new kind of music absolutely repellent to the adherents of the older dispensation, and that the process was repeated when this new style yielded to its successor. We find, further, that no "new" style can be looked upon as a "throw-back" to some earlier type. Thus we have in Music a form of thought which in its evolution presents marked crises, occurring with such definiteness that we may interpret them as analogous to periodic climaxes of constructive energy, but with this difference that they occur decades and not centuries apart.

There is in this clearly a parallelism with nature's plan as regards the physical properties of life. Our knowledge of biology has been arrived at largely if not entirely by a study of comparisons. The behaviour of one form of life under specified conditions leads to the investigation of the influence of a like environment on other species more or less akin to it. A group of phenomena observed in connection with one phase of life may cause a search to be made in order to ascertain whether the occurrence is unique or whether it has any bearing upon other phenomena which await explanation.

There is no such thing as an organism completely insulated. At some point or other it makes a contact with the life-current. Every accidental offset in nature, every "sport," has to be studied with a view to discovering wherein it conforms with accepted types. The scale of evolution is a vast staircase, leading to various habitations, but yet uniting them all, and it must be trodden if we are to cross their thresholds.

Bearing in mind the hostile attitude assumed by one School of Music towards the newer one that seems to tamper with its preconceptions, and remembering at the same time that Music has advanced only by a courageous effort to break with superstition, we see that we must always be readjusting our standard of excellence: we are compelled at every turn, no matter how reluctantly, to admit the validity of new claims, and to recognize the consistency of new methods of procedure. Music is a young art, and there is no outward expression of man or of nature to which it can be referred for verification. There are, it is true, instances in the graphic arts which show an effort to cast aside convention, but even these are to be reconciled with some broad principle which explains, if it does not wholly justify, the effort towards independence. Now in Music all the greatest effort has been towards this independence. Without it there would have been no Music, and it is the due recognition of its existence that we have to keep ever before us. Music essentially is Revolt: the time is not yet for the gentle folding of the hands. But violent as its upheavals may be, they cast down no landmarks, they dislodge no coping-stones. These remain as the highest standard of the art at the time when they were erected.

In the brief history of Music there has been a re-adjustment of values such as no social code, no system of government, no art, indeed, has seen. In this present generation we have been compelled, not once but many times, to correct our focus. The architect, the sculptor and the painter all profit by the experience of their forerunners in their art, and it seems difficult if not impossible for them to evolve a theme or style of treatment which has not already been anticipated in some instances centuries ago. Each no doubt has to pass through stages of mental development not unlike those of some great predecessor, but with this difference, that he has not been forced to think out the problems which confronted the artist of an earlier period. He, in fact, was working in a plastic medium and was moulding his art: the artist of to-day is occupied in moulding himself.

Freely conceding that there are conspicuous examples of great sculpture and painting in our own time, and recognizing the accomplishment and insight of numbers who belong to the modern period of art, we must not lose sight of the fundamental truth that Sculpture and Painting are mimetic, and no matter how far the artist can remove himself from the bald facts of his theme, he starts from an actuality and, insensibly it may be, is guided by the experience of his predecessors as to the manner of projecting into his work his own personality. Individuality then asserts itself in the instinct for conceiving a theme and selecting the best means for fulfilling the conception. But no matter how fresh the point of view may be, or how "original" to modern and possibly uninstructed eyes, it nevertheless may be but a reflection of something equally great if not greater, carried out at a period when the obstacles and difficulties were infinitely more formidable because they had to be encountered and overcome without any aid—without, in other words, the support gained from the experience of others. Upon this experience is tradition founded, and tradition, handled by man, varied, improved, dissected and considered from all sides, becomes strong enough to afford us a standard of excellence.

As regards Music the standard is far more a personal one. We have rather to consider some isolated individual taste than any broad and general acceptance of a principle. Whatsoever is new in Music cannot be referred to a type which has come to be accepted as unassailable in the light of experience. The composer has to be weighed, not by a hard and fast rule which stands for all time, but by an unstable, fluctuating, variable standard which estimates not only his actual accomplishment, but also the state of development of the art at the time when he produced his work. In other words, the intrinsic qualities of a composition may be influenced and determined by the extrinsic conditions.

It would be no feat for a composer to write another *Orfeo* to-day, with his faculty developed through the knowledge and experience of composers since Gluck; but practically every bar of a modern music student would have been a gigantic achievement had it been written in 1762. It is not a question of the convention or the idiom of the time: it is rather a sign of the art advancing towards maturity through one brain after another, each adding something that was beyond the imagination of the preceding generation.

CHAPTER III

HISTORICAL BEARINGS

In order to appreciate the various stages through which Music passed before it reached its present condition, we have to consider it in its historical perspective. It is needless to discuss the theories that have been advanced as to the origin of Music or its "usefulness," because in the last two hundred years immense changes have taken place, not only in Music itself as an expression of mental energy, but also in the creative faculty of the composer and the receptivity of the listener. In other words, there has been a change in Man, the immensity of which we can best comprehend by a brief retrospect.

Upon one point, however, I must be emphatic. I am not here analyzing the æsthetic value of any given composer's work, but the mental endowment which he has to possess before he can produce that work.

The records of musical notation stretch back for

nearly three thousand years, but if the human faculty of Music were suddenly to vanish and nothing remain except these records, we should still be able, not without immense labour however, to put them in their order of evolution, regarding them as parts of some obscure problem the key to which was lost. The growth of Music as an organism is so definite that we can mark off each step as we ascend the scale, allotting this or that characteristic with some degree of certainty to its appropriate period, and classifying a composer or a school of composition as we would some form of animal or plant life. We should not hesitate till we reached the last, the present stage, in which the "proliferation" has taken place with such immense rapidity as to defy systematic analysis.

We are not concerned, in this part of our study, with abstruse questions. Carrying our minds back to the tenth century of the Christian era we find Music still where it had been for twelve hundred years. The earliest piece of musical notation extant is cut on a marble slab, and is known as the Delphic Hymn to Apollo, ascribed to the year 278 B.C. Our knowledge of Greek music is not derived from existing writings or inscriptions in musical notation—these scarcely amount to one hundred bars—but to various treatises which have come down to us. Researches may yet bring to light evidence of harmony, but nothing of the kind has been found.[1] We have no notion what this music actually was, for a theoretical discourse upon it may have been merely an ingenious form of dialectics, but that there was music in some form or other in the daily life of the Hellene there can be no doubt. The Greek mind, however, busy with all that concerned the intellect, could not be satisfied with that which was sung, and codified the notes of the scale, defining the sense and purpose of each according to the note with which it began. Hence the Greek modes, which were transmitted orally, through one vicissitude after another, till twelve hundred years later, about the year 900 A.D., it occurred to some one, purely mechanically, and, probably accidentally, to add a second part to the tune.

Wholly apart from the matter which we are investigating, the importance of this cannot be overestimated in any study of the human mind. We are only able to realize it by some forced analogy, as, for instance, by imagining a digital system of five integers, which persisted till a very recent date in the Christian era.

In the tenth century, when a rude attempt at harmony came into existence, men were so captivated with the new sounds that they used them indis-

[1] The subject is more fully discussed in *The Threshold of Music*, ch. iii.

criminately, whether the effect was good or bad. We may indeed question whether the ear actually did distinguish harsh from pleasant combinations of sound, seeing that the mediæval theorists worked very much if not entirely by rule of thumb, and constituted themselves the authorities as to what Music was to be long before the infant Harmony was weaned.

It is of importance to note at this point the immense difference between the capacity of the musical faculty in those days and at the present time. Without any special training we feel the necessity for harmony to give a melody completeness, and the intrusion of a discord affects us physically as well as mentally. This sensitiveness appears to have been wholly absent in the period under discussion, for the harmony that pleased the earliest theorists is primitive and frequently intolerable to us.

It is not surprising that a system of harmony which was hedged about with all manner of restrictions made very slow progress, and even by the middle of the fifteenth century there was little evidence of the mind being conscious of sounds which could be used in combinations other than those laid down by rule.[1]

We need not examine each step in detail, but it is

[1] "It is impossible to doubt that the art of accompanying a melody by chords (as any amateur can now do in the simplest manner possible) was completely unknown to musicians up to the end of the 16th century."—Helmholtz: *Sensations and Tone*: Lond. 1875, p. 245 *b*.

important to note that with the relatively large number of minds occupied with music of all kinds, engaged in the contrivance of instruments, and formulating theories as each stage in the art was reached, it took the musical faculty seven hundred years to bring harmony from its embryonic state to the maturity upon which our modern music is based. Even if we make every allowance for convention, there can be little doubt that the ear of man in those times was very different from what it is now; for although seven hundred years are ample for many conventions to be established, enforced, and ultimately derided, they do not account for the extremely meagre results that were gained from century to century.

Human energies, perhaps, were being expended in other directions, but in Music men did not seem to be thinking or striving to hear for themselves. They appeared content to accept the precepts of their age without testing them in the crucible of their minds. We do not find any deep manifestation of individuality. There was scarcely a sign of consciousness that Music might be carried any further than the stage at which each new-comer found it, and while the expert may detect minute differences which enable him to assign a particular work to one School or another, on general lines there was no startling departure, no innovation to disturb the leisurely and complacent advance of the art.

It is not germane to our argument that great works were written then and still exist: what we have to note is that composers, with the exception of Monteverde, showed none of that desire, so characteristic of modern times, to break away from convention,—none of that impatience with restraint which has advanced the art so rapidly in our own day.

The most significant feature of Music even as late as Beethoven was the slightness or total absence of individual development, and this doubtless had much to do with its slow progress. When we come to Bach, who is looked upon as the founder of modern Music, we do not find him undergoing any marked development as he advanced in years. It would indeed be difficult to single out a work of his which differed conspicuously in treatment and theme from those written at an earlier date in his career. It is a striking fact that no contemporary of his and no immediate successor reflected his influence. He may often have gone back to his earlier work and rewritten much in the light of an enlarged experience, but his mental equipment was so sturdy, so independent, and above all so personal, that he began as himself and ended as he began. In other words, he never "lost his accent," and owed little of it to others.

He was the first to demonstrate that Music was a form of thought. A great deal that he wrote was an intellectual conception without special regard for the means used to interpret it. There are many passages which could never have been played in his day, and seldom in our own, by the instruments for which he designed them. It may be that in his mind he had a fanciful timbre associated with some instrument and found the mental result so complete that he did not trouble to ascertain if the music could be practically reproduced. The marvel is that this giant should have sprung from a race of pigmies, for round and about him in his early days there was no commanding intellect in Music that could have stirred his ambition and driven him forth to seek new worlds in sound. It was as if he had heard much and thought for himself, not suffering fools gladly, but assimilating from all till he designed for himself the plan of his life, and then set to work to erect the spacious hermitage where Music might find sanctuary.

The art is not yet old enough to point to another Bach, and our passing circumstance, dominated by a plethora not of brains but of wits, hurried on by a crowding, as it were, of leisurely years into one frenetic day, may dismiss that necessary interruption, that little pause, when Nature draws back and takes breath the better to leap forward and get to business again. Nature undoubtedly did leap forward to give us Bach, and possibly from sheer exhaustion or from surety that the thing she had made was good, possibly from secret joyousness of having wrought a wonder, lay still and watched man's next effort.

But Bach was dead ere the next in the heroic line came to be born, and it was Nature's humour to keep out of sight for a space that which he had left behind. Bach's immediate influence upon Music was nil, for it was only forty years after his death that composers turned seriously to his works to preserve them from oblivion. He had brought a technical branch of the art, counterpoint, to its last stage, and there was not among his successors that deep interest in him that is shown to-day, for the reason that he stood apart from the doings of smaller men and lived out of the current. So it is that in coming to Mozart we have to seek his god-fathers in art among the minor prophets. It is not without significance that he and Joseph Haydn should have shown no individual development as one work followed another. It is inconceivable that a composer, at the outset of his career, should display such maturity as to be incapable of further development as he grew older, or should be so completely detached from all external influences as to continue his course unswayed by outward occurrences. No one more than the composer of later days has been susceptible to the tides of the world, and his development has been progressive. At the period under review, however, we have to consider the special circumstances that gave rise to music.

These were Opera, the Church, and the private Patron. The composer who had to earn his daily bread was not in a position to assert himself in an unequal contest. Hack-work and drudgery gave him a little security, but even these were unstable props if he wished to count upon the due recognition of his gift, and he could not at all times escape the charge of pot-boiling.

Whether the patron was a Bishop, an Impresario, or a Grand Duke, the composer was not always at liberty to follow his own bent. The singer, too, had often to be studied and conciliated, and had a good deal, perhaps rather too much, to say when his part came to be written. The result was that a considerable amount of the composer's work was cast in the same mould, and when one composition succeeded in pleasing the patron, the composer repeated himself as far as his self-respect would allow. He may have been cursed with a facility for turning out music, which, though it might show no haste or carelessness, was nevertheless too artless to be looked upon as a serious and deeply considered effort.

It may indeed be asked if facility in composition is not wholly antagonistic to stability and permanence. Many a work endures which was written rapidly and at the cost of no apparent effort, but the survival of one work produced in this manner does not meet the question. The facility at this stage of musical history must have been enormous. Boccherini, in a period of activity of about forty-five years, produced 467 instrumental works, not to speak of vocal pieces. Of them all, practically only one little minuet has kept his name alive. Yet he must have enjoyed much popularity in his day for eighty per cent. of his works got into print. A century is too short a time in which to decide what of a man's work will live, and we cannot forecast the verdict of a future generation upon Haydn's 150 symphonies, and Mozart's 40.

The absence of personal development may be accounted for by the nature of the music itself. The human faculty had not evolved many new ways of doing things in music: it was content with old formulæ: the composer's powers of creation were not taxed unduly. Orchestral music in its higher forms, such as the Symphony, was descended from the old Suite, itself a simple elaboration of a string of dance measures, and the transition was obvious and not a little trite. The composer had always at hand conventional and mechanical aids when he was at a loss. Arpeggios and scale passages kept many a movement going long after its interest had ceased.[1]

There was little evidence of that anxiety which

[1] "Scale passages especially annoy me: suggesting that the composer, 'gravelled for lack of matter,' runs upstairs to find an idea, and being disappointed comes down again."—Herbert Spencer in *Facts and Comments*, Lond. 1902, p. 81.

Beethoven was to show so pathetically, to hammer the theme into shape so that it should fit the plan of his thought. Many themes consisted of little else than the notes of the common chord of the key in which the movement was written, and when they had been somewhat extended, the usual padding began.

Much of this music is charming, with a slightness and superficial prettiness; but it may be asked, particularly of the orchestral music, whether a great deal of the mental impression produced upon the listener is not due to the absence of any arresting quality and to the perfection of performance, while the sense of hearing is paradoxically suspended as he watches the conductor.

Apart from the material of the music, Haydn and Mozart had a conception and appreciation of design which was deeper than any to be found in the work of their predecessors, Bach alone excepted. The wonder is that Mozart should have been content to end as he began. To say that he entered the world with a mental endowment so perfect that it could gain nothing from human experience is the kind of assertion that puts the investigator on his guard. A moment's thought will demolish such a claim. Mozart's lack of self-development may have been due to some of the causes already mentioned, such as the outward circumstances of music, but probably also to the absence of the right kind of stimulus.

A child made so much of as he was in aristocratic circles could not shake off as he grew older the early habit of mind acquired by contact with others dwelling in a sphere so unlike his own, and there may have been somewhere in his mind a complacent satisfaction that as he was already so different from other men there was no need to widen the gap.

It is the man and not his music that we are considering, but unfortunately we have no contemporary observer who has left records of an aspect of character which at the present day has assumed considerable importance.

This conception of design to which reference has just been made is often encumbered unnecessarily with a confusion of musical terms: the simplest explanation is to be found in the every-day expression, "a sense of proportion," carried in this instance, not into life and living, but into Music.

Later on we shall have to consider an important part of the composer's equipment, and that is the faculty of accumulating his thoughts mentally while he creates, bar by bar, so as to preserve a just balance between the various sections, and to take care that there is no incongruity in the elements of which the work is composed. Mozart possessed this gift to perfection. Even the artificial devices of which he made free use, puerile as many of them may strike us to-day, had their purpose in giving the mind a moment's pause, thus delaying what was to follow and preparing the listener for some new theme which in those days might have appeared arresting and unconventional. For everything in Music at one time was new. The modern composer dare not resort to the Mozartian formula, and chooses rather to carry the development of the theme much further than Mozart actually did—what Mozart might have done does not concern us.

His contribution to the evolution of Music, then, was not so much technical as it was æsthetical, and the art entered upon a new stage by demanding of the composer a higher intellectual effort than the one cultivated by the acquirement of knowledge.

When we come to Beethoven we find, so far as we know, the first conspicuous example of a composer undergoing self-development, while at the same time adding new "characters" in his evolution. His early work was imitative of Mozart's, but when he began to think for himself the traces of Mozart's influence disappeared. Still, even while that influence persisted, there were suggestions of that Beethoven idiom which later was to assume so vast a shape, and these beginnings were sufficiently pronounced to show how dominating was his power of self-expression from the very first.

As far as we can infer from the music at our command, this self-development in the composer came about little more than a century ago, and it is a striking characteristic of the more recent phases of musical evolution that every composer has undergone the process. Thus Music at last has been brought into step with the march of the intellect.

Every composer since Beethoven's day has shown a desire to create in music something that was wholly out of reach of the musical faculty of former times. It would not be fair to assume that he is falling back upon sounds rejected by those of an earlier generation, for they had been taught to follow the text-book rather than their own instinct, and had they heard deeply and felt strongly, they, like Beethoven, would have made the text-book follow their instinct.

The text-book of to-day bears the relation to modern Music that an English grammar does to *Paradise Lost*, for the composer is striving to utter what he and he alone hears, without any concern with the dispositions of the book-men. The musical faculty has come into line with other imaginative processes, and the composer will at length, if he is not already doing so, write music as a language that he commands as easily as the poet does his mother-tongue. For the construction of the framework, for the technical knowledge of his instruments, he must necessarily pass through much schooling, but the profound act of composition cannot be taught.

A composer, with the natural gift fostered by his

surroundings, can express his ideas by relying upon his ear long before he has studied the bare rudiments of music. This was the case with Mozart: there are many instances. But most bewildering of all is the young musician who, without having heard any modern music, and without having had access to it, shows us a composition demonstrating an "advanced" phase of musical thought. What is to be done with him? Is he to be sent to the nursery of grammar? The responsibility of guiding such a mind is great, and ought not to be entrusted to those whose sensibilities have become blunted or atrophied by inelastic methods of education.

It is precisely this mystery of the mind that is so little considered or studied,—this delicate and complex machinery of thought that is, as it were, at the mercy of some heavy-handed blacksmith who beats out on his anvil that which is right for the dull hoof, but is not fitting for the sensitive mouth.

In spite of the progress that Music has made in our own time, we are still as far as ever we were from solving its mystery. We may regard it as a special language used by some to express their thoughts, but nothing is of greater significance than the fact that, widespread as its appreciation may be, it has not yet escaped from the leading-strings of its alphabet. Its content is so little understood generally that the musician, in discussing a new work, has for the most part to fall back upon points purely technical in their interest. In the case of works which we have studied and assimilated, we unquestionably receive an æsthetical and emotional stimulus, though we may not be able to describe it. But in listening to these compositions the musician cannot divest his mind of thoughts of the mechanical details that attract his attention as the music proceeds. No art is wholly proof to this objective analysis, and Music in particular suffers and must suffer, because its nature compels the composer to carry in his mind a vast knowledge of the capabilities and limitations of the means upon which he relies in conveying his thoughts to others.

We have to inquire into that knowledge and its application to the cultivation and development of his special gift.

CHAPTER IV

INDIVIDUAL DEVELOPMENT

In the foregoing chapter we considered somewhat rapidly the progress of the music-sense through the ages. The survey was necessary, for although the historical aspect of the art has been discussed by many writers in the fullest detail, its relation and application to the march of the musical faculty have not hitherto attracted the student to any great extent.

Reference was made to individual development, and we have now to consider this large question not only as it concerns the composer but also as it affects the auditor.

It will scarcely be contested that the material, the substance, of music has undergone a great change in the past century. Some would ascribe this to the better understanding of the orchestra, and this is partly true; but in music dependent upon a fixed and constant means for performance, such as chamber music, pianoforte music and songs, the assertion cannot be maintained. Were we to express the construction and elements of an extended orchestral movement, for example, the First Movement of Beethoven's C minor Symphony, in terms of a formula, apart from any emotional or æsthetical content, we should have something like this—

$$a + b = b + a$$

$$ab + c = c + ba$$

But with our present musical knowledge this simple formula would not serve to enunciate the plan and pattern of the majority of modern works.

It cannot be said that the older composers were invariably satisfied with a form of utterance which strikes us often as ingenuous, or that they deliberately eschewed the complexities which we find in modern music. Some, indeed, appear to have been content with a minimum of effort, but of this we cannot be sure, for they themselves may have considered their work as a deep and intense expression, outweighing that of their contemporaries in strength and amplitude. We have grown so accustomed to a riot of material in modern music that we cannot comprehend the critical indignation of the contemporaries of an older school which they expressed towards a kind of music that sounds naïve nowadays.

Music indeed is still in want of a standard and a tradition. Many a hasty opinion arrived at in a moment of expansion has called for revision because of the development of the art. It is not that some of the geese were swans: some, if we are to believe all that we are told, were eagles: some even peacocks. The judgment of contemporaries many a time has been reversed by a later generation, and the dictionaries teem with the records of composers who in their day enjoyed great popular favour, but have now become merely objects of antiquarian solicitude.

Whatever the tendencies of the art may be, or however deplorable the results may seem to many, we must never forget that we ourselves are in a state of transition, and that what was good for our grandfathers may not be good for us.[1]

We may therefore hazard the conjecture that each generation has the music that it can just comprehend, the fuller understanding coming with the succeeding generation.

Our own transition is easily demonstrated when we compare our attitude towards music which was new to us some time past with our opinion of it now. Had we lived a century ago, the contemporary music might not have appeared so simple an affair as we consider it at the present day. The mind that is receptive keeps pace with the art as it is evolved, stage by stage. The individual that as a child was

[1] "It is no exaggeration to say that the universe was not the same for our great-grandfathers as it is for us, and that in all probability it will be utterly different for our great-grandchildren."—Pearson: *The Grammar of Science*, p. 15, Lond. 1900.

brought up on Clementi, may, through the Romanticists, have his mind prepared for the idiom of Wagner, and by cultivation be led to a high degree of appreciation. If he still keeps alert and gifted with divine curiosity, he is in a state to comprehend further developments. But should he find himself unable to follow or even to condone the latest phases of his own time, it is not logical or consistent that he should brand them as corrupt. Had he been born 150 or 125 or 100 years ago, he would still have assumed the same attitude towards the last and most extreme utterance in the music of any of these periods.

To canonize the Strauss of the Symphonic Poems and to consign to darkness him of the Operas is merely to acknowledge that the mind that understood the earlier phase has not moved forward to grasp the later one. It may be objected that no allowance has been made for taste, and the old adage rises in one's mind, but is not taste a faculty that can be developed just as it may become stagnant? The amateur of to-day, who refuses to consider as "Music" anything written since 1830, overlooks the part which the music which he derides may have played in instructing his faculty so as to appreciate Bach or Beethoven. So delicately is the mental apparatus adjusted, and so gently and imperceptibly are the currents guided that it is not always possible to recall the moulding of a thought.

Many an idea can be analyzed amid the frequently incongruous ramifications that led up to it, but we do not know what part the music that we dislike or condemn may be playing in the formation of our appreciative faculty. It is true that in striking and memorable instances a profound emotion has sunk so deep into our experience that we can identify and piece together the links in the chain. In music we can sometimes call to mind all the circumstances connected with an instant when we were intensely moved, and, possibly later, can laugh at ourselves in a phase which we have outgrown. But as our musical faculty advances—not towards maturity, for that never can be attained—we shall better allow for the exuberances of our youth, for these, in the process of development, must have been associated with a less highly organized form of music. The mind that has accepted an advanced form cannot, except when atrophied, revert to a primitive type.

As Music has progressed from stage to stage, and as the horizon of the creative faculty has widened, the receptive faculty has also moved forward. The law of supply and demand has been reversed: it is the supply that causes, or rather brings about, the mental condition which feels the necessity for the demand. We are not concerned with any economic question here: let that be understood. Man devises an abstract form of thought which at first is incomprehensible to his hearers, but constant repetitions of similar forms of thought compel them insensibly to adjust their minds so as to appreciate, if not fully to understand, the new idea that is projected towards them. They have their minds ripened for the cultivation of new forms, and the development proceeds.

This transition is characteristic of the composer of modern times, as has been suggested in the last chapter, and when scarcely a week passes nowadays without a "star" of as yet undetermined magnitude blazing into space, each with some rare, or borrowed, effulgence, we are frustrated in our attempts to locate it.

Music as we understand it has not yet established her Eternal Verities.

The conditions of the art have always been favourable to transition, first at long intervals: now startlingly sudden. As one period has overtaken another, every composer has benefited by the experience of his predecessors, and has turned to his own advantage all that he found was new. At the present day all are out in the world to make discoveries, but Time alone will discriminate between the sincere of purpose and the mountebank; between the charlatan and the poet.

The possession that has passed into the treasure-house of mankind is beyond price: the composer's heritage is boundless. Packed into a mere afternoon of 150 years we have an art individualizing itself with such potency and vitality that we are able to assign special characteristics to this or that composer with some measure of certainty, and when we examine these characteristics we find that they are not normal in their development, but are often directly in contradiction with those of their immediate forerunners. Further, we have no signs of atavism : there has not been time for such a throw-back to occur. Instances spring to the mind in which we believe we may detect some degree of atavism in living composers, but we cannot claim them as indisputable examples until we see upon what lines they will develop.[1]

The pedigree in art of the great composers is a brief one, and we follow it back without difficulty, but it is singular to note how very little evidence remains of what one composer owed to another. Wagner had the extraordinary gift of selecting from the thoughts of others just that leaven which was necessary for his own. Hence we have him turning from Mozart to Beethoven, from Weber to Meyerbeer, from Berlioz to Liszt, and yet there is not a trace of any of these composers in his mature work. His work indeed is like some organism puzzling the biologist at various stages of its life-history, now

[1] The atavism here referred to is not physical but mental and artistic. The best modern example is the Pre-Raphaelite Movement.

inclining to this type, now to that, and in the end shooting forth into something totally different from any foreshadowed in its course.

Herein lies the unique character of Music—the more bewildering when we consider the limited range of tones with which the composer has to work.

The paradox has to be admitted that individuality in Music is begotten of influence, and that the composer is constituted a "type" when, after having shown at each stage of his development the influence of other "types," he ultimately emerges as a "neoplasm" with every step in his pedigree obliterated. What community of thought, we may ask, had Bach with Monteverde? In the scale of chronology we find odd neighbours. Brahms was born nine years before Arthur Sullivan and predeceased him by three, while Tschaikovsky, a contemporary who was intolerant of the one and very likely wholly ignorant of the other, corresponded as to years with both. The three had the same Old Masters to study, their education in Music was orthodox, and there was nothing unusual in their surroundings; yet their individuality of style could not have been more marked. Wherever we turn we find this characteristic of the prominent composers that they prevented anything like a tradition gaining a firm hold upon their art; on the contrary, had tradition become established in any strength, it would have stayed their progress, and we might have had from Wagner nothing but Symphonies in the manner of Haydn and Mozart, and no one but the adventurous would have dared to disregard the canons which convention would have prescribed. Even then he would have found himself in antagonism with the "tradition of the elders," which, if we read our history aright, was scarcely on the side of progress.

In the earlier days, when Music was in its infancy, it was being developed in minds that timidly responded to the stimulus conveyed by the intelligence of the age, and sought hesitatingly for an individual means of expression. Thus there was no arresting difference between the work which a man produced in his youth and in his maturity. He ended as he began, maintaining a just level of accomplishment, and making for himself and his patron music that was uninfluenced by extraneous currents of thought. This was not evidence of a tradition. Rather was it that the musical mind had no conception of the vast domain that was to be explored: it was still in a state of childhood, unable to grasp the potentialities that lay beyond, and satisfied with what could be accomplished without great effort.

This is typical of composers up to the last quarter of the eighteenth century, and is in strong contrast with the continuous development of the man as well as of his art that is so conspicuous to-day. The earlier composers did not seem to realize the magnitude of their work or its ultimate destiny in the affairs of mankind. Their method appears to have been determined by the circumstance that called their music into being; and there was little anxiety to know if Music might not be in itself a circumstance. The growth towards a style was slow. There is a vast quantity of the older music that might have been signed by one man instead of by a dozen. Innovations were made tentatively and with diffidence owing to the array of prohibitions laid down by the schoolmen.

With the coming of Mozart and Beethoven Music entered on a new phase, and we have for the first time in any marked degree one composer exerting a definite influence upon another. This indicated some points of importance. It showed that there was a style sufficiently well established and characteristic to appeal to the composer, and that he was aware that it was worth studying and cultivating. Its value to him, further, was clear, for he was founding his work upon a model that had been tested and accepted as the highest that had then been reached. Although he was following in his early work the lines that had been laid down by his predecessors, he had the consciousness that as he gained experience he would ultimately secure a mode of utterance that was individual. It showed, above all, that the composer deliberately sought after the last stage in the development of his art, and that whether he had considered the matter for himself, or was following his musical instinct, he was adding his own link to the chain of evolution.

The "etiquette" of Music had come to an end.

It is particularly the case in Music, an art in which the fundamental canons of what is good and sound have yet to be determined, that almost every composer who has made a name has passed through the assimilative stage; he has absorbed all that he can of a style that can be traced back, step by step, through his own development. His instinct guides him to select the medium in which his musical thought has widest play, and his position in the hierarchy depends on the amount of his own personality that he can project into his work.

Therefore when the remark is made that some young composer has begun where Brahms, let us say, left off, we dismiss it as the ill-considered and uninformed criticism of a man who has not applied himself to the study of the mind and its workings, or to the life-history of the great composers.

This catching up of the thread from Brahms or from any other composer may be deliberate or unconscious, but it is undoubtedly a step forward in the progress of musical evolution. It is a sign that the composer realizes that he too may have something to say, for he is working in a fluid medium not yet confined within accepted limits. What next will be said in music baffles the imagination, for it will depend in creation and appreciation upon the development of faculties beyond our control and beyond our foreknowing. Doubtless in time to come archaistic Schools of music will arise and revert designedly to styles that were the fashion in days gone by. That has been the experience in other arts, even as far back as the age of Pericles. The reproduction of music typical of a past period is constantly done at the present moment in order to obtain local colour, but there has been no widespread movement towards a former type, and it is most unlikely that music written by a modern composer on the formula of Scarlatti would find any acceptance.

In order to have this continuity there must be, in the first place, a form of musical thought of sufficient strength to stand forth and be identified by its characteristics.

In the second place it must have vitality to impress a mind predisposed to come under its influence. If we call this second mind the "receiver," and the other the "generator," there must be present in each certain similarities. What these are it is impossible to define sharply; they may be purely physical or purely psychical: they may be a combination of both. It is probable, however, that the "receiver" is attracted to the "generator" by some emotional quality in his work, or even by sympathy with him in some accident in his life which the younger man imagines is paralleled with one in his own.[1]

While individual development is essentially a characteristic of the modern composer as distinguished from his predecessor of a century ago or even much later, it is not present in all in equal strength or in a uniform rate of progress. Verdi, who had used for close on fifty years his own stereotyped idiom, assumed "new characters" when many thought that his life-work was done, and amazed the world by enriching Opera with a fresh quality.

Mendelssohn, on the other hand, was almost in the fullness of his powers when a mere lad, and underwent little development in his career. It was his misfortune to be the predominant influence of his day, unrivalled for his facility and the meticulous "toilette" in which he arrayed his ideas. Like Mozart he had the utmost command of musical expression. Never at a loss, never compelled to reconsider or reconstruct, he poured forth an even strain of music which scarcely varied in its finish or its dexterous nicety.

He was the supreme musical mind of his day, and

[1] Many a girl has gone on the stage, not because she could act, but because her friends thought she was the "living image" of some popular actress.

cast his spell over his contemporaries. But in the development of their musical faculty we should have expected them to explore new realms of sound, bent on making discoveries for themselves. This they did not; they merely imitated their master, with much of his facility and deftness, but, like him, they lacked the adventurous spirit. Their world was complacent, unwilling to be disturbed by the intrusion of a new idea which insisted upon hard thinking, and it accepted the pale reflection as the genuine creation.

There are, consequently, exceptions to individual development, and they are to be found when a composer shows in his early years a precocious maturity. Music in such cases is self-centred and self-contained. It is a manner of thinking in itself, unrelated to and uninfluenced by any outward circumstances or other trains of thought. It does not attempt to illustrate or suggest an idea which can be expressed by other means: it depends solely upon its own content, and grows and expands from within itself.

The composer whose musical gift is of this nature is able, intuitively and without much technical instruction, to write works in the larger forms rivalling the compositions of others of wider experience than himself. But it seems to be the case that he undergoes little development, and the works that he produces as he grows in years do not vary widely from those of his earlier style. He may be influenced by the tendencies of the day, but only so far as they happen to fit into his own mode of expression, and they are absorbed so completely by his habit of thought that their presence is not detected.

Much of this may be explained by a consideration of the surroundings. A composer whose ripe gifts declared themselves in his youth was more likely to attract notice than one whose work cost him effort and deep concentration, and who developed slowly. Few are the cases in which the faculty for composition showed itself at an early age, and those who possessed it won recognition almost before they were out of their teens. It was difficult to escape the temptation, once the public ear was gained, to exercise this natural ability which came without much exertion, and to continue the steady production of music which made no revolutionary departures.

Nowadays this attitude of mind is not encouraged. The composer who did not put forth his strength and show that his work was advancing would lose ground. The leisurely ebb and flow of ideas which served at earlier periods have been displaced by violent oscillations so rapid that the mind has not time to note the beats. Composers in a more placid age were not affected by impulses and movements within their art, rivalry was slumbering, there was no frenzied egotism that drove them to seek for originality in extremes. They were much in the position of painters who were content with a superficial view, and aimed at depicting what others were likely to understand rather than what they themselves saw.

This placid outlook had a suspicion of time-serving: it came perilously near the brink of pot-boiling, but a simplicity of purpose and a child-like sincerity disarmed censure. The readiest and uppermost thoughts were accepted without searching analysis.

The modern composer finds himself in very different circumstances, and though the conditions are more disquieting, they provide a more potent stimulus. The constraint of external influence has to be taken into account, but the freedom of imagination which at first made for success may lead to a weak surrender at the dictates of some publisher or critic. Thus the making of a composer may be his own undoing, and those original qualities which counted for his salvation may be blunted by concessions to popular taste, or sacrificed to win some doubtful and passing approval.

The composer, however, whose freedom of action is not to be bought or sold, is in another category. In his mind his art is not so insulated that it is unaffected by other currents flowing around him. The artless, and apparently thoughtless facility of a remoter day is disregarded for it conveys nothing to him. At the same time Music is not to him mere journalism, and though the ephemeral mood may hypnotize those whose aim is to attract attention rather than to bring others into their orbit of thought, his experience strikes deeper.

As his mental growth develops, his musical growth cannot be arrested, and although his work may not be the literal reflex of every change of circumstance in his life, it shows the increase in his knowledge with the added weight of time and endurance. His personality, therefore, is projected into his work, not indeed with some trumpery ascription to an outward influence, but in a soberly considered and mature form.

The trials of the past, galling as they seemed, now justify themselves, and the acknowledgment of their necessity, of their teaching, takes the edge off their bitterness. These make for growth and especially for self-criticism, ere the memory be numb and the mind cease to be alert. Thus it is that in the organic Music of our own time there is not that vain repetition of threadbare formulæ which passed muster when Music was feeling its way in men's brains, clinging to the broad roads for fear of losing itself in narrow and winding tracks. It has gone on adventurously in search of those hidden by-ways which, as we now know, lead to great discoveries in the hills and valleys of grey matter.

CHAPTER V

THE WONDER-CHILD

If we were to draw hasty conclusions from the fact that on the interpretative side of Music amazing instances of high technical skill are found in young children, we might be disposed to accept them as evidence that Music as an art is on the lowest plane of all. It might be argued, for instance, that because some children are able to perform on musical instruments with an accomplishment far outstripping the efforts of many an adult, the acquirement must be easy and simple.

Instances of precocity in the other arts are not rare. They are least numerous in Sculpture, possibly because the materials are not always within reach. In Painting, thanks to the attention given to the training of hand and eye in early childhood, large numbers of small boys and girls are able to sketch from the round with an accuracy of technique and observation which has ceased to be remarkable.

More striking is the imagination and inventiveness which have been found associated with a strong feeling for colour and the human figure. As time goes on, it will be a point for careful study whether this faculty, when met with in a child under ten years of age, does not become attenuated at twenty through sheer exhaustion, or the fear of doing things incorrectly, which often is the only result of rigid discipline in the schools during the intermediate period.

As regards this a digression may be permitted, for the matter is too important to be dealt with in a foot-note. It concerns the training of the child as much in general subjects as in art. It has just been said that unusual gifts in the graphic arts and in Music may be displayed at an early age, and a grave responsibility is undertaken by those who have the direction of these gifts. In schools of the fine arts and of Music, where a hard and fast routine prevails, it may happen that much that a child does unconsciously and without instruction may seem to him utterly wrong at a later stage when he is left to himself, and he may deliberately suppress and discard the very qualities in his work that gave it freshness and spontaneity. Thus the child who sketched through intuition and happiness, whose line was unerring and free, may be so terrorized by that overaweing and enervating tradition of the elders, that his work loses all its hope and elasticity, and becomes, as the phrase runs, "as hard as nails." It is right that many novices should "go through the grind," but it may be noted that in these typical expressions associated with education, there is no hint of a clear understanding and appreciation of the difficulties of childhood, no earnest of kindly and gentle guidance, but instead, the language, if not the menace, of tyranny. Is all this wise?

A child does not master French or Latin by intuition, but he may have a gift that causes his teacher some heart-searchings in secret. It will be urged that a system, a carefully-ordered curriculum, cannot be upset because of the exceptional pupil. That well may be so, with parents and guardians single-eyed, but if the exceptional pupil is to grow up into the one just man, it would be to the eternal glory of a school if it put guidance before restraint. Let it be clear that no plea is entered here for irresponsibility and conceit. When it is a question of education in any branch of art, faults in character are infinitely more serious than defects in technique. The student, if he has an atom of the artist in him, will do his utmost to correct imperfections that concern his art: he will give the go-by to those that touch him as a man. It is disaster when the young and gay mind, like a happy tree in spring, conscious of its blossoms, is ruthlessly mutilated by those who are careless of its fruit.

Precocity in the arts is seen in its most highly organized state in Music, and the results are the more bewildering when we take into consideration the processes involved. In drawing and painting the child is mimetic: he can copy some one else's copy: he can be taught the direction of a line: he can be shown how to rectify an awkward foot or shoulder. These are technical matters, and of course are entirely beside the imagination in his work, but they are referred to here to suggest the possibility of "touching up" by a more experienced hand. This cannot be done in a musical performance. The child of eleven who plays the Brahms Violin Concerto in public cannot be aided by anyone: the effort of memory and technique are absolutely his own: and he has before him forty minutes of intense concentration. It must be confessed that the mystery is inexplicable. What is there in the construction of the child's mind to enable him to display a mastery which many adults cannot attain even after years of study? What is there in his sensori-motor system that overcomes technical obstacles? How is it that the violin, the most difficult of all instruments, is found in the hands of young children, whose correctness of ear and intonation whose precision of muscular movement, seem almost miraculous?

Although cases of this prematurity are more frequent than would be supposed, the number of those who come into the public view is small,—smaller still the number of those who maintain their talent at a high level throughout their lives. The gifted children of past days may have reached a creditable old age without fluttering the telegraph dials, but at the present time, when even the most humble being may suddenly become the terminal of a machine which transmits trifling events, it is impossible for an unusual occurrence to escape notice for long, and as the prodigy has a definite commercial value it is not likely that his talent is allowed to rest under a bushel.

It may be that extreme endowments in a child were formerly overlooked, although musical history supplies accounts of those who displayed marvellous ability at an early age. It may be that hidden away in some Balkan fastness, in some forgotten purlieu of an inaccessible Slavonic village, or in some Ghetto of ambiguous suzerainty but indelible lineage, there was many a tiny performer who amused himself with his instrument and was the joy—perhaps the butt—of his playfellows.

Possibly we now hear of these children more frequently because of the facilities which their exploiters possess for bringing them into notice, and if we inquire into the nationality of these young performers we find that many have a strong Israelite strain. It has often been asserted that those of Hebrew descent fill the ranks of the musical profession to a greater extent than those of other stocks. To verify or deny this would be difficult without an investigation entirely outside our present study, but we may consistently ask if it is not the case that they probably seize every advantage conferred by the presence of a natural gift, and recognize in it a means to an attractive and highly coloured life; while others, not of Hebrew parentage, are disposed to treat their musical gift as of secondary importance and apply themselves to some career which seems more utilitarian in form. It is to be remembered that it is the executant who is under discussion. The vocation that can be pursued by the exercise of a natural gift, without too much study of extraneous subjects, has a fascination for men in certain worldly circumstances, and it is not surprising that among foreign executants we meet with many whose general education has been of the scantiest. This applies to individuals of all ages, and its bearing on what follows will be evident.

The parent of Eastern Europe who belongs to a lower stratum of society has none too many scruples about making use of his own or anyone else's child so long as he can profit thereby. If the concert-room is not available, there is always the café chantant, the club, in fact, to which he resorts, night after night. Thither he takes his child to play for the benefit of the company, with a few coins as his reward. Some stranger happens to look in, and struck with the child's performance, and not quite oblivious of his own advantages, hints how the parent might improve himself. The rest of this part of the story is simple.

If we keep this in mind, never forgetting the all-important fact that the child in the East of Europe comes to maturity four or five years earlier than he of the West, we have one explanation—not the only one—why talent does not, and is not allowed to declare itself publicly at an early age in those born on and beyond the left bank of the Rhine.[1]

The average Englishman, for instance, has a horror of the imputation that he is living on the earnings of some one else, particularly on those of his own child. The feeling is not peculiar to one class, and public opinion has been strengthened by legislation on the subject of child-labour. At the same time there is to many people something disconcerting if not painful in the spectacle of a child barely in his teens displaying a command of an instrument, entirely apart from the question of emotional interpretation. They feel that

[1] Age is not a matter of years, but of physical development, and the standard under ideal conditions should be a physiological one. In spite of their prematurity, many foreign child-performers are under-sized when they reach manhood.

this ability testifies to large sacrifices in other directions, and their thoughts are engrossed less by the performance than by the circumstances that rendered it possible.

There is another point. The educated man, no matter what his nationality may be, is alert to the future. He has no intention of offering his son as a hostage to fortune. Where the prospect of a liberal allowance is remote, the question of a vocation which will bring in an immediate return is an urgent one. The choice of a livelihood becomes of the utmost importance, and when parental resources are fluctuating, a career which carries a pension with it is at the moment the most attractive. Whether the son is of the same mind, either then or in later life, is not a matter which we have to go into here.

From these general considerations we return to the child-performer, dismissing nationality, environment, and artistic and commercial prospects, and weighing only the mental aspect of the question. It is clear that no matter how musical the child's parents may be, they can do little more than instruct him in the technique of his art. He has to develop himself from within, and as he progresses, his parents, hearing reports of the fame of other wonder-children, turn his talent to account. Many of the great instrumentalists made their first appearance before their fifteenth year, and special care was taken with their artistic education from the moment that their unusual talents were recognized. Many had mastered their instrument and their public before their schoolfellows had got as far as a jews' harp.

It is scarcely possible that at such an early age they could have possessed the mental qualities necessary for interpreting without help and advice the infinite varieties of emotion and feeling which Music can express. The mimetic faculty, so strong in the child, must have been exercised to a very large extent by patient labour over details and by incessant repetition of isolated phrases, in order to obtain an authentic and consistent rendering.

But while this led up to the moment when the child faced his audience, there was something else in the course of the training which was beyond any human interposition or influence. What we have just discussed is the last stage through which the child passed before he made his first appearance. It is unquestionable that it must have demanded unwavering perseverance, but all would have been thrown away had not the child shown definite natural aptitude for his task, and it is this which is the most important element which we have to study.

No one can master an instrument—as in the case of a great performer—without being intensely predisposed through some prematurity, or abnormal development, or hyperæsthesia of the centres of the brain which control the muscles of the hands. Mozart at six, Liszt at nine,—respectively the ages at which they made their first appearance in public,—must have had a different calibre of brain from von Bülow, who had passed the age of nine before he began to take an interest in Music, and was twenty before he released himself from the harness of the law and espoused the cause of Wagner.

Much as we should like to attribute to romantic surroundings the germination of the artist, in the child we find an accidental capacity for performing certain muscular acts, which, when applied to a piece of mechanism like a pianoforte keyboard, can evoke sounds and convey auditory impressions to the listener.

This may be a bald statement, but it goes to the root of the question.

Let us examine these muscular acts. The keyboard of a pianoforte is contrived so that each key has its own note at a fixed point in the scale. We know beforehand what will happen if we strike one or several notes. On the finger-board of the violin it is different. It is not marked off into sections so that a non-musical person can produce a given note. Its sections are invisible, but sought for and readily found by the trained violinist, who knows to a nicety on which part of the string to place his finger. In addition, within certain limitations, it is possible to produce the same note on more than one string. The absence of any indication as to the points at which a string must be pressed in order to produce a given note with the bow makes it difficult for the beginner to play in tune, and unremitting practice is necessary to bring the fingers to that degree of sensitiveness when they find automatically their relative positions.

The minuteness of adjustment will best be understood by the layman by a reference to the restricted area in which the four fingers of the violinist's left hand move in order to span the compass of the instrument. The finger-board of the violin is about ten inches long, gradually widening from three-quarters of an inch to one and five-eighths of an inch. Its area therefore is less than thirteen square inches. The same compass extended in a straight line as on the piano keyboard measures about twenty-four inches by four inches in width, giving an area of ninety-six square inches over which the ten fingers move. As the space for the fingers on the violin is so narrow, it will be evident that the utmost delicacy of touch is necessary, and that the slightest error in the position of the finger-tips will produce an unpleasant effect.

The pitch of the instrument has to be regulated by the performer, and one of the earliest stages in his development is the training of the ear, so that he can tune the four strings correctly without reference to an instrument such as the piano, whose pitch does not vary. This constant determination of the pitch and tuning of the strings, establishes in the mind a fixed point from which all note-relationship can be obtained. It further educates the ear so as to recognize in an instant the slightest divergence from correct intonation. Thus we have the first essential, a true ear.

The complex acts which must be performed in order to produce a series of sounds are the result of manifold impressions calling forth muscular movements of extreme intricacy, and when these movements are repeated at ever increasing degrees of speed, the will that controlled them in their first stages ceases to influence them consciously, and they discover for themselves their own exact rhythm and order. This is the second step, and, like the first, it is reached by training and cultivation.

But there is a combination of the first and second which cannot be explained so simply. Some people have what is called "knack," by which is usually meant a ready adaptability of their muscles to perform certain acts. Whether the existence of a "muscular sense" has been recognized or not, it is unquestionable that some individuals have a remarkable control over their muscular system which others undoubtedly have not, and that this control seems to be a special endowment apart entirely from training. It is met with commonly in sport, and the display of many accomplishments in this sphere of activity counts for much virtue. In art, for some illogical reason, versatility incurs disapproval, as if it were reprehensible to exercise the brain as one exercises the arms and legs.

This "knack"—the word is not used in a derogatory sense—is not infrequent in musicians, who appear predisposed by some unknown means to the performance of mental and physical acts connected with their work. It is probable that they are endowed with an unusual combination of the elements which go to make up the so-called muscular sense, and that the muscles themselves are in a high state of sensibility.

In medicine the *tactus eruditus* is priceless ; but though the hands can be trained to something approaching it, it is doubtful if they can be brought to that refinement of accuracy of touch and extreme delicacy of control which are found in those who have the good fortune to possess it. It appears to be a quality inherent in the individual.

Instrumental playing may be described as a series of impressions which result in voluntary actions, and these, by constant repetition, become instinctive. The brain, through the eye, recognizes the printed note, and puts in action the muscles that are concerned with its production on the instrument. The hand voluntarily seeks for the part of the key-board that it has been trained to associate with the printed note, and the special movements, dependent upon the character of the instrument, are performed.

The printed note, the recollection of its sound and pitch, the sound-thought in the mind, provide the stimulus, and each through its appropriate channel affects the nerve centres which control the muscular movements that are to be brought into play.

The nature of instrumental playing will be better understood by a reference to the act of writing. This at first is laborious: the mind has to guide the pen at every stroke: it has to think of every shape and turn in the formation of a letter, and it is long before the voluntary act becomes automatic. This can be tested by writing with the left hand. The experience of the mind as regards the rapid and involuntary movements of the right hand is concentrated upon those of the left, with disappointing results, for the muscles of the left hand have to begin with the same mental and muscular attention to letter-formation that was exercised in the case of the right hand.

It will be obvious, from the example of writing, that a series of studied and considered muscular movements can merge into one that is muscular and voluntary only in a sense, and also that the faculty of muscular discrimination and selection can be developed. Such movements, with all their dynamic varieties, become completely reflex while the mind is riveted upon the performance, that is, while the perceptive centres are being violently stimulated.

Expert performers on musical instruments develop this faculty still further when playing unfamiliar music; they "read ahead." In other words, while their hands are playing one bar of the printed music, their eyes are taking note of the contents of the next bar or two, so that when each successive bar is reached, the brain has already determined—"made up its mind," in fact—how it is to be fingered and played.

As exemplifying the translation of the voluntary into the automatic act we may turn to the experience of men in the habit of delivering a fixed series of lectures. Many an audience has been absorbed in and fascinated by the periods of a speaker, who, were he to tell the truth, would admit resentfully that he had been wakened out of a beautiful dream by the applause at the end of his discourse. On the stage, during a "run" which may occupy the greater part of a year, this automatism is inevitable. A curious instance was related to me by an eye-witness who, as a member of the orchestra, was intimately acquainted with the play. An actor and actress, both of them clever and popular, had a scene together, which, after some 250 performances, had become automatic. The scene was amusing, and rounds of applause followed at definite intervals. These interruptions occurred so regularly that the actors invariably waited till there was silence again. But on one occasion a point missed fire and there was no applause. This was so unexpected and disconcerting that the pair completely lost their bearings and had to leave the stage.[1]

It would be fascinating to trace these manifestations further, but we must return to the child. Their import, however, will not be lost in the special case of the young instrumentalist. Whether or not we call it "knack," we cannot say more than that in gifted children there is a hyperæsthesia of brain and nerve machinery, possibly too of muscle machinery, which produces extraordinary results.

Although the names of notable child-performers can be recalled, there are not so many who reached maturity and continued in the fullness of their powers till past middle age. As we shall see later,[2] we have to depend greatly upon the biographical dictionaries for information, supplemented by personal observation. Many talented children, through their relatives or agents, have courted public favour just a little too soon, but have not succeeded in retaining a hold upon their audiences when they reached manhood. Their work has fallen off in adolescence, and has not been

[1] Wagner relates in his *Life*, vol. i. p. 361, that at the reinterment of Weber's remains at Dresden, he made his first speech in public, delivered by heart after careful preparation. He was so carried away that he fell into "a sort of trance," and seemed not only to be listening to himself, but also to be seeing himself in his surroundings. A long pause at the end of a sentence reminded him that he "was not there to listen but to speak."

[2] See pp. 134, 136.

deemed worthy of notice in reference-books. These are particularly the cases which would have been instructive in an investigation into the stability and permanence of talent displayed in childhood, but they are passed over because the impression that they created was transient. Again, in the case of performers of the first rank who had reached adult age before they challenged public attention, we do not know to what extent they practised self-suppression before they felt assured that the moment was ripe for their first appearance. We do not know, besides, how far the wisdom of their guardians and teachers restrained them from entering upon their public career till every step towards success had been carefully thought out. This wisdom, too, may have struck deeper with the knowledge of the evanescence of popular approval and taste, and, forewarned, his friends may have shielded the wonder-child till he had grown up, ready for manhood's garb and its burden.

In the prodigy, then, we find a highly receptive and sensitive musical faculty, but one which seems to be largely unconscious. He does not realize the magnitude of his performance, and consequently is not deterred by the obstacles which in older people would give rise to anxiety and nervousness. We might almost say that the will—the centres of volition in the brain—are suspended, and that the act of performing is mainly reflex, in a large measure external to, and independent of, direct thought and concentration.

In support of this view we have the fact that the child-performer has always outnumbered the child-composer. The child-composer is rare; Mendelssohn, who was a marvellous performer as a child, is one of the very few youthful composers whose earliest works still find a place in modern programmes, and who ultimately reached a prominent position.

The very young composer has to exercise faculties entirely different from those which are essential to the performer, for he has to fix his attention upon the sounds that he is writing, and to think how they may be most effectively combined.

The child-performer often has a brief public career, although there are notable exceptions. In Mozart and Mendelssohn their continued efficiency as performers was due to their creative faculty for composition keeping their minds on the alert, and leading on and sustaining their interpretative faculty. In other words, the unconscious element in their work as pianists in their childhood was converted into a volitional act under the influence of the more potent stimulus of composition. Similarly in the case of Joachim, his modest excursions into the world of composition forced him to apply to his violin-playing the thought and study demanded by composition, and enabled him to develop his powers of interpretation.

The special aptitude for violin or pianoforte playing, when manifested at an early age, tends to exhaust itself as the child grows up. Many brilliant performers, now in their maturity, who began as prodigies, may appear to refute this statement, but, fortunately for them, their circumstances and environment diverted their attention from the exclusive course which they had been pursuing as interpreters, and caused them, as men, to take note of and consider the larger aspects of their art. Possibly too their intercourse with other musicians, particularly in modern times, when there are so many compositions seemingly written with a view to incite discussion and dissension, forced them to study the tendencies of their art in order to guard their own position. Thus they were compelled to recognize the existence of many other affairs in Music outside their own restricted field.

Modern conditions of life, also, may influence this continuation of the interpretative faculty. The talented offspring of parents in a humble rank of life has now more than one continent at his feet, and since the journey from Prague to Chicago nowadays can be performed in less time than was Haydn's classic trip (as we should call it) from Vienna to London, there are sights and scenes that keep his attention on the alert, and the constant variety is enough to make him older than his years. Some change must take place in every child subjected to these conditions, the more so if he has found his vocation at an age when other children have hardly begun to dream of theirs.

We may sum up the physiological aspect of the question by assuming that in the child-performer there is a hyperæsthesia of the sensori-motor tracts when connected with the reflex-auditory centres, and that this hyperæsthesia tends to become exhausted unless the tracts and centres are brought into circuit with volitional centres.

It has already been suggested[1] that when creative powers are shown at an early age, they present themselves in so mature a form that they do not expand, and scarcely deviate from the style and accomplishment that first won their recognition. This seems to be true of executive powers also. It is conceivable that as he grows up, the child may lose that faculty of concentration which in his early days was an instinct more than a deliberate mental effort. His unusual gift may enable him to overcome difficulties too easily, and when he begins to appreciate that they *are* difficulties, he may shirk them or his nerve may fail him. We have to bear in mind also the possibility of his character deteriorating through publicity and adulation,

[1] See p. 56.

while the high tension at which he has to live is bound to bring about a reaction. There are influences in his life from which there is no escape, and he may ultimately pay too great a price for a gift which descended upon him at an age when he scarcely grasped its magnitude.

The most inscrutable problem of all is the origin of the emotional quality which the child conveys by his performance. A good deal no doubt is purely mimetic, and he may simply reproduce the teaching and experience of an older mind. But his own musical intelligence and appreciation must to some extent keep pace with his technique and expand with it. A common criticism is that these children play like children, but it seems to be influenced by objective and not subjective considerations. The mature musician is able to put into his work his personality, his intimate thoughts, his deep knowledge, and whether we agree with his reading or not, we feel that it is something more than a superficial and conscientious regard for the composer's indications and nuances.

One aspect of the child's ability to suggest the emotional content of the music that he plays must be taken into account, and that is the possible influence of the audience.

Of late years there has been much speculation as to the extent of this in connection with matters unrelated to music, and there are instances on the public platform of discordant demagogues falling to, or beneath, the level of those whom they are addressing, and abandoning themselves to a line of thought (if that is the correct description) utterly at variance with their conduct in other places. We do not know how much is due to the audience, but this mode of utterance cannot be attributed to purely intellectual qualities. Again, the comedian who feels his audience with him experiences an irresistible impulse to improvise, to "gag," and public speakers in their happiest efforts have been stimulated by the attention of the meeting.

These are examples of a performer or speaker dealing with arguments or sallies which occurred to him on the spur of the moment, and the sympathetic attitude of the audience may in some unknown way have reacted upon him. The element of "personality," also, must not be excluded, but this is a large question of itself.

With music the conditions are somewhat different. We do not know if a child plays better in public than he has done during the preparations for his appearance. The context upon which his performance is based, the notes themselves and the composer's indications, do not vary, but we are unable to say how much of the interpretation is due to the surroundings and the presence of a large number of people. We do not know, further, how far he may modify his "reading," as his elders do, upon a momentary impulse which throws a new light upon a passage.

These are questions which cannot yet be answered; it is sufficient to conjecture that in time to come a close connection may be shown to exist between the emotion of the audience and the emotional responsiveness of the performer.

It is a common phrase that this or that performer or speaker "swayed" his audience, but we are not yet in the position to assert or deny that it was he who was "dominated" by his listeners, who came in a mood of receptivity and appreciation, and departed after hearing the wonders that they expected and were prepared to hear.

The power of "suggestion" hitherto has been regarded as the influence of an individual over others, whether singly or in mass; but if its existence is accepted, there is no reason why an audience should not possess a collective form of mental activity which is concentrated upon the speaker or performer.

This possibly anticipates future developments, but the forecast, purely imaginary as it is, may yet be confirmed. For the present the most we are permitted to surmise is that in the mind of the child-performer there is something else, apart from all schooling and rigid discipline. What that is no man knows.

CHAPTER VI

FUNCTIONAL CHARACTERS

THERE is no known mental process which resembles Music: the composer's special faculty is the most mysterious with which man has been endowed. We can conceive of no explanation why the intellect should busy itself with the orderly succession of sounds, from the simplest tune to the most complex symphony,—why it should conceive these sounds, meditate upon them, and give them forth, not because of a utilitarian demand from without, but in obedience to a pent-up inner force which clamours for freedom and expression.

We might try to imagine what existence would be for us were all Music to be excluded from our lives. Some other faculty of creation and appreciation might possibly arise, to be developed in directions which we cannot foresee any more vividly or wisely than the composers of the middle ages could have anticipated the extent to which Music was to grow. The question cannot be answered by the assertion that civilization would be the worse without the presence of that mental force which in recent times has demanded so large a share of man's interest. To say that Music is an emotion is not to answer one question but to ask a myriad. When the problem of its usefulness arises, and when we seek to connect it with anything in our own experience, we are unable to find a solution. No sentimental explanation is of avail: Music may leave us in a happier frame of mind: it may touch the highest and the deepest within us. But why should it? Why does it?

We are not at a loss in the other arts. Except in extreme cases we are not out of sympathy with the sculptor and painter, for we understand the medium in which they work and can confirm the results from our own knowledge without in any way intruding upon that domain of their art where their experience leaves us behind and no reign is acknowledged except that of their personality.

In Music, however, the composer works in abstractions, and though, with our own trained musical faculty enlarged and expanded, we can say whether the thought strikes us as being well expressed and elaborated, we are able to follow him only for a short distance on the long road that he travels.

We now pass to a part of our inquiry which is purely speculative, and accordingly we are compelled to make large assumptions.

Reference has already been made to the reluctance of scientific men to discuss this psychic province of the brain. This is comprehensible, for almost instinctively they confine themselves to the sphere of determined fact. Obviously we cannot do this here, but without indulging in far-fetched theories we can make some comparisons.

We can prove nothing, but we can imagine everything, and while we have all the joy of hazarding conjectures, it is none of our business to verify them. Scientific truth is merely the confirmation of a hypothesis.

1. *Physical Comparisons.*

The ingenuous remark of a Dutch anatomist[1] who flourished at the beginning of the eighteenth century may be taken almost in a literal sense as a warning to those who, 200 years later, attempt to connect the musical faculty with the minute anatomy of the inner ear. It may be said at once that an anatomical study of the auditory apparatus in man throws no more light upon the composer's special endowment than an investigation of the retina does upon the art of the painter.

[1] "Multum laboravi ut hæc ossicula cum membrana timpani in situ naturaliter delinearentur, sed pene impossibile est: quorum tamen descriptio mihi videtur potius confusionem quam scientiam paritura."—Verheyen: *Anat. Hum. Corp.* Lib. i.; apud Coloniæ, mdccxiii.

In daily life our auditory judgment of itself is extremely limited as regards the distance and direction of sounds: in identifying these it is compelled to rely upon the aid of the other senses and upon experience. The musician in this respect is no better off than others who have not trained musical faculties, but he has, as part of his equipment, an individual power of analysis which, in the case of writers of orchestral music, has been brought to an extreme degree of sensitiveness.

It may be that civilized man has lost certain auditory properties which at one time were essential, and, as will be seen presently, we are very far from understanding nature's plan in the disposition and protection of the inner ear.

In tracing the faculties we must ever look back and try to arrive at the way in which intelligence dawned as the reflex of the senses.

The sense of hearing is the last to be suspended before sleep supervenes. In primeval days the sense of smell may have served for defence, and through the development of the faculties it may have become attenuated; but in the darkness of night man had to rely upon his ear alone for a warning.

The primary necessity was the means to sustain and preserve life, and to keep the foe at bay. So long as there was light to see, the track of enemy or prey was evident; experience noted signs friendly or hostile, and daily life was regulated accordingly. But in the night, except for some few hours in the moon's appearances, the vision was of no help. Some other sense, therefore, had to be cultivated to make the homestead secure. Man's hearing was not limited by the rising or the setting of the sun. Unlike his vision, it did not depend upon a periodic disturbance of the ether : it was continuous and lasting and was influenced by vibrations proceeding possibly from the same source, but transformed into a different form of energy.

While he lay sleepless he could count the stars and have his quarrel with the moon, but the crack of a twig close by whipped every muscle tense, and the brain put into action its power of analysis to interpret, according to lessons bitterly learnt, the personal meaning of the sound.

In some respects man may not have varied, but we have lost, or at any rate we are not now endowed with the protective ear-instinct to the extent that is still to be found in primitive civilizations.

It was remarked at the beginning of the chapter that the retina tells us nothing about the painter's art. But a comparison of the senses of sight and hearing is useful in demonstrating some striking points of contrast.

As regards vision we have the exact science of optics to elucidate certain processes, up to, but not beyond the great Barrier which we must always face. We are further aided by a knowledge of the physical principles of light and the properties of lenses. The eye itself can be examined minutely; measurements can be made in certain diameters to the fraction of a millimètre. Its condition in health and disease can be directly observed, and its morbid anatomy studied under the most favourable circumstances. The course of the optic nerves can be traced and their ultimate distribution noted with surety, for nature has here withheld from us little beyond the last process of all,—the means by which the brain is stimulated to the perception of light.

When, however, we turn to the ear, we find the auditory apparatus entrenched behind an impregnable bastion, so that the investigator can see merely the portcullis, as it were, while all the inner works are concealed.

We are unable to see the apparatus in action, and are driven to theory to account for every step following the impact of the sound-wave upon the membrane of the ear-drum. Various theories have been advanced as to the functions of the Organ of Corti, but although these are of the utmost scientific value, they throw no light upon the present inquiry. Nature's purpose in protecting the auditory machinery so completely is obscure: research has shown that a part of it is concerned with functions which have no apparent connection with the sense of hearing, and it is unquestionable that behind the membrana tympani lies a vast world yet to be explored. The outward defences of the apparatus are a mystery. We do not know if at one time the organ possessed some faculty now lost which would account for nature's precautions, or if one is yet to be developed which will explain the measures for resistance which we find disposed with incomprehensible forethought. πολλὰ τὰ δεινά, but nature still has her secrets.[1]

Some other points have to be noted at this stage. Theoretically the visual act is complete only when both eyes are in combination. The visual field for each eye—the area that is perceived by each eye separately—is limited in certain directions owing to the projection of the nose, cheek, and eyebrow.[2]

[1] With the exception of those more intricate parts of the brain which are out of the surgeon's reach in life, but can be examined without difficulty immediately after death, the inner ear is the most formidably protected part of the body. The compact nature of the bone in which it is situated and other technical obstacles of an anatomical kind, which need not be detailed here, often prevent the histologist from obtaining in the human subject the material for his study readily and in a fresh state. His microscopic preparations have for the most part to be obtained from lower mammals under conditions which are not always ideal.

[2] In his *Researches in Colour Vision* (Lond. 1913, p. 191) Sir William Abney still plots the field as ovoid, using the ordinary pattern of perimeter. But "by the rotation of a double-image prism held close to the eye, an apparently moving object, the reflexion of the fixed object, is seen. The area can thus be estimated in all

Each eye separately has one part of the visual field in common with the other eye, but the part of the field which the right eye cannot see owing to these projections, is visible to the left eye, and *vice versa*, hence one eye supplements the other. Each accordingly has its own separate image of a portion of the total field, and the total field becomes visible when these separate images overlap exactly and thus become fused.

Without entering closely into anatomical details we must note this intimate relation of one eye to the other. There are further points. Both sides of the brain are simultaneously stimulated by each optic nerve proceeding immediately to its own side of the brain and partly to the other. An accident involving the "dangerous zone" of one eye will most certainly affect the other unless stern measures are adopted, while a serious lesion of one side of the brain may affect both eyes.

Another point of importance to us at this stage is the automatic occlusion or suppression of the secondary image in certain errors in the refraction or optical adjustment of the eyes. It has just been said that

directions independent of any obstruction to the luminous rays from projecting adjacent parts." Measurements taken with a specially constructed instrument showed for the first time that in normal cases "the field extends nearly equally on all sides round the fixation point."—The quotations are from my Thesis, *The Field of Vision, etc.*, presented to the University of Glasgow, 1888.

the separate images of each eye coalesce, so that the mind is conscious of only one image. But when one eye differs from the other because of an error in focal adjustment or some other defect, two images are seen, as for instance in the case of squint, and this is popularly and correctly called "seeing double." But as these two images are confusing, the brain has the power to select the image that is the more perfect and useful, and to disregard the other.

It is possible, as we shall see later, that this power of selection may be present to some extent in the case of hearing.

So far as we know, this intimate relationship between the eyes is absent in the case of the ear. We are not able to say whether one ear supplements the function of the other, either as to range or delicacy of perception, but we have the two auditory organs recording the same impression, so that we hear one sound. The two sounds therefore coalesce, just as the two visual images overlap, and thus become one.

The anatomical distribution of the auditory nerves is much more independent than it is in the case of the optic nerves. It is only their terminal fibres on either side that reach the opposite hemisphere of the brain, and a lesion of one auditory nerve does not necessarily involve the other.

But even when a lesion does exist, resulting in complete loss of hearing on one or both sides, we have this important fact to note that the trained musician who suffers from this impairment, while he is shut off from the world of sound, is nevertheless capable of using his musical faculty, as we know in the case of Beethoven, Smetana, and Robert Franz. This shows that the psychic centres for Music are independent of the auditory apparatus in trained musicians, but the music written during deafness has peculiarities owing to the composer not having been able to hear his work aloud by testing it at the piano, and also to intra-auditory phenomena. This is recorded in the case of Smetana; in his string quartet in E minor it is asserted that a "persistent high note in the finale is understood to be a deliberate statement concerning a note, similarly persistent to his own ear, which was the effect of his deafness."[1]

Beethoven furnishes a similar instance in the Finale of his Choral Symphony. Here the voices sing for the most part at the highest point of their compass, and the sound to many is anything but pleasant. It would be interesting to see whether among musicians who become deaf, there is any tendency to force up the pitch.

This independence of the psychic centres for Music will be dealt with later when we come to consider Mental Audition.

A further difference between the eye and the ear

[1] *Grove*, 2nd ed. vol. iv. p. 486a, *sub v.* Smetana.

may be mentioned. We can occlude the sense of sight at will, but we cannot cut ourselves off from sound. The faculty of Inhibition is not here referred to: it will be investigated later; but it is sufficient to say that the voluntary suspension of the faculty of hearing is beyond our powers. Local Authorities that so readily suppress evil smells see no necessity for putting a stop to evil sounds, and the curse of street "music" may have as disastrous an effect upon the nervous system as bad sanitation has upon the physical health. The ear has no power of self-protection, and he who would have his lodging sound-proof would need to dwell upon a mountain, and even there to reckon with the eagles.

Meagre as the foregoing appears to be, it is practically all that concerns us as regards the bearing of anatomy and physiology upon the musical sense.

At this point it is convenient to consider some general characters.

The mind is developed by experience, and experience is memory.

The individual acquires knowledge from impressions which are converted into perceptions, and these as they accumulate, become memory.

Thus we form a mental diagram. We may assume that a new impression of which the individual has had no former experience results in an unusual grouping of brain-cells in order that perception may take place. When the impression is repeated, it is reasonable to suppose that the same grouping of cells will occur, and with further repetition will become constant or habitual.

For example, I hear a musical phrase in an unfamiliar timbre. I am told that it is produced by a new instrument with which I am not acquainted. I am shown the instrument and learn what its compass is, what are its good and bad registers, what restrictions there are owing to its mechanical construction, and so forth. The first time I hear the instrument it is probable that an unusual grouping of cells is stimulated, and this results in a new perception. When, however, it is repeated, I recognize it because my perception of its character has been established through my recollection of its timbre, and also by inter-association with a number of other perceptions which have stored up all that I have noted about the instrument and its possibilities for my purpose. My mental perception of the instrument having become constant, I am able at will to hear its timbre mentally, and with concentration to combine it with other timbres which through experience are fixed in my mind.

We thus get a definition—there are many—of experience, which, in this connection, is the perception resulting from a large number of stimuli.

If we accept this as a possible, but always theoretical explanation of a single operation of the musical faculty, we may construct much upon it. The single operation, let us assume, consists of a combination of a number of other operations, for in order to arrive at perception I have used my discrimination by instituting a multitude of comparisons based upon my memory and experience.

I am not attempting to make a mystery of the process: I am merely suggesting the likely course which an auditory impression might take.

The transformation of the unusual into the habitual is at the root of all musical development. When once the unusual has ceased to be new, it passes into the common currency of thought.

So far we have been summarizing the result of external stimuli. We now have to consider the act of musical thought when the theme springs into the mind, either in a rudimentary form or perfect in its content. Every composer has endured weeks of torture owing to the persistence on the edge of his mind of a tune which he cannot define clearly. He is unable to "visualize" it distinctly. He hears mentally, but the effort to realize the precise form of his thought, that is, the musical sound, fails because the cells are not in complete circuit. Other groups not usually in combination must be brought into the circuit before he can grasp the thought. This grouping, having been established, will then remain constant.

When a musical theme arises spontaneously, unassociated with any external stimulus, we assume that it is due to the fortuitous combination of a number of cells not usually linked together. The unusual combination creates the unusual thought, and by exercise and cultivation the new circuit is continued. If this be so, it will readily be understood that at the moment when the unusual circuit is completed, and before it becomes permanent, some external stimulus may destroy it, and this will explain why, in all forms of brain-work, but particularly in Music, the whole of the delicate adjustment may be thrown out of gear by an interruption, such as the opening of a door.

In those who bring great concentration to bear upon their work, it is probable that the unusual cell-grouping can be brought to some extent under the influence of the will, so as to be maintained unbroken for long stretches of time, for weeks or even months. Thus a habit of thought may result from a purely accidental combination of cell-groups.

The power of resistance will be discussed presently under Inhibition.

2. *Mental Audition.*

It is one of the many paradoxes that we meet with, that music can be independent of sound, and that musical sounds can be recorded visibly. It has already been pointed out in the case of Beethoven and other composers that serious impairment of the auditory apparatus did not affect their creative act, although the music produced in the period of their deafness showed certain characteristics. The perceptive centres, it would appear, are not absolutely dependent upon the auditory apparatus, but these centres could not have been developed without the "ear" having been at one time highly sensitive to external musical impressions. In his earlier days Beethoven heard as other men; under normal conditions there was in his case an intimate connection between the action of the inner ear and the perceptive centres, and when this connection was abolished these centres continued to act with the same vitality. This indicates that when the mind had established in circuit, as it were, the centres necessary for or involved in the creation of music, it became independent of the mechanism of outward hearing and the activity of these centres persisted. Thus we are able to affirm that the realizing of music mentally and in silence must be preceded by the perception and appreciation of audible sounds. From this we infer that the capacity for Music is "acquired,"[1] and depends upon conditions external to the individual. Its persistence

[1] The importance of this will be evident when we come to consider Heredity. See pp. 135-6, 156.

in musicians who ultimately become deaf is due to the mental factor having been firmly established before the external auditory functions became suspended.

An interesting light is thrown on the subject by a consideration of the cases of Laura Bridgman and Helen Keller, who, as is well known, became deaf, dumb and blind in infancy, that is, before they had begun to speak or to understand the meaning of words. Thanks to a system of education which in itself was a miracle of patience, observation and resource, their minds ceased to be abodes of darkness and silence. When Laura Bridgman (1829-1889)[1] reached the age of twelve she began to keep a journal, which, we are assured, was literally transcribed, the only alteration being the introduction of capital letters. In the earliest entries we do not find any mistakes in spelling, and such words occur as *brought*, *deaf*, *dumb*, *learn*, *see*, *teach*, *taught*, *rode*, *night*, *flies*, *eat*, *show*, *comb*, *reach*, many of which a child of the same age would be inclined to spell phonetically. In her poem, "Holy Home," there is a good, probably reminiscent, choice of phrase, but no rhyme or metre or assonance.

Helen Keller[2] wrote her first letter a few days

[1] *Laura Bridgman*, by Maud Howe and Florence Howe Hall. Boston, U.S.A.: Little, Brown & Co., 1903, p. 84.

[2] *The Story of my Life*, by Helen Keller. London: Hodder & Stoughton, 1903, p. 145. She was born in 1880.

before her seventh birthday. We are told that everything has been[1] "preserved as Miss Keller wrote it, punctuation, spelling and all." I give her first letter in full:

> "helen write anna george will give helen apple simpson will shoot bird jack will give helen stick of candy doctor will give mildred medicine mother will make mildred new dress"

A hearing and speaking child of that age would be in difficulties over *write*, *george*, *apple*, *simpson*, *mildred*, *medicine*. It will be noted that there is not an assonance or rhyme in any of the words. Less than six months later (pp. 148, 149) she managed *photographer*, *vegetables*, *build*, *pigeons*, and *wednesday*, that stumbling-block to the illiterate. At this time she remembered *heliotrope* and *chrysanthemum*. In her letters at the age of eight we find *mon cher monsieur*, *parlez-vous français*, *oui*, *vous avez un joli chapeau*, and the following Greek words, printed in the text of the *Letters* in Roman italics: *se agapo*, *pos echete*, *kalos*, *chaere*, *kale emera*, *kale nykta*, and—*theater*, which betrays her nationality.

In each of these cases words were not arrangements of consonants and vowels implying sounds, but ideographs as the French non-phonetic words show, while the Greek words demonstrate the limitations

[1] *Op. cit.* Part II. *Letters*, edited by John Albert Macy, p. 144.

when a language is written "out of" its own characters. The value of a study of these instances lies in their proving that mental audition does not exist unless the auditory faculty has been in contact with actual sounds, and unless the individual has been of an age and intelligence to grasp and appreciate and store them in the memory.[1]

The discrimination between one timbre and another, such as is necessary for orchestration, depends on the memory, associated with the power of receiving external auditory impressions, and it would be impossible to teach a congenitally deaf person the infinite shades of tone that are met with in the modern orchestra, especially those which closely resemble one another though they are produced by different instruments.

A deaf man, who in his happier days had made himself familiar with the characteristics of instruments in their timbres and combinations, might write for them effectively without producing an unpleasant tone. A point worthy of the fullest investigation by those who have to deal with defects of hearing is the raising of the pitch, which has been mentioned earlier

[1] It is scarcely necessary to point out that anyone can master a non-phonetically written language like English, French or Modern Greek without being able to understand it when it is spoken. To a vast number of persons our present musical notation conveys no more than the *Sa-Ri-Ga-Ma* characters of the Indian sol-fa scale do to occidental musicians.

in the chapter. In his days of enforced silence, Beethoven wrote passages which we feel sure he would have reconsidered had he been able to hear them. Presumably he was satisfied with them as he heard them mentally, and this seems to indicate that his eye did not assist him, or rather that he was convinced of the correctness and "practicability" of the passages because they represented what he was hearing in his mind. He may have firmly believed that he was carrying Music a stage further, or lack of critical judgment might explain the inconsistency, but we know that of all composers none was more self-critical than he.

Mental audition is not specially confined to the province of Music. We hear mentally while we read in silence, suspending or suppressing our articulation during the act. In committing a phrase to memory we articulate each syllable, but the consciousness of this action varies in individuals. Similarly in the transcription of a passage, the consciousness of repeating each syllable is present in different degrees, as also is the act of spelling in the use of a type-writer. These acts by experience and practice become more or less automatic, but the sound of the word is often present in the mind, sometimes so positively that an assonance, or "jingle," or repetition is detected although a considerable distance separates the words concerned. The actual sound of the first word, therefore, persists in the mind without the agency of the auditory machinery. In technical subjects, owing to limitations of the vocabulary, there is no escape from this repetition.[1]

The assonance that has just been spoken of is met with in music, and is characteristic of vocal phrases in operas of the Italian school, in which one note in the scale, usually the dominant, persists with irritating frequency. Another form is the use of the same note in a phrase or chord on a strong accent in two or more consecutive bars. A further weakness, to which all composers must plead guilty, is the repetition of a phrase at the beginning or in some part of a melody.

Mental audition is of the first importance in the composer's equipment. In many instances it is simply the specialization of a function that everyone possesses in greater or less degree, and one, further, which can be cultivated. Most people can hear a tune "in the head," without sound-waves acting upon the tympanic membrane. It occurs as a reaction to many psychical

[1] The painstaking avoidance by Macaulay of a repetition or an assonance at the distance even of a page was pointed out some years ago by a writer in an American magazine. He made an interesting and elaborate study of two editions of the *History of England*, comparing Macaulay's revisions with the text of the first edition. The reference unfortunately is lost. Against this sensitiveness of ear may be placed the laboured efforts of some writers to call common things by far-fetched names.

stimuli, and does not depend upon the co-operation of the auditory apparatus in those whose hearing is normal. Complex as the process is in all individuals, it is specially so in the composer, who familiarizes himself with signs and symbols of definite significance. These signs, according to their variety and scope, convey a mental impression of rhythm, pitch and timbre. If there is a single series of them, as in a melody, the ear can realize the harmonies that accompany the notes, and when notes and harmonies are written down, the ear, guided by the eye, can hear the chords and detect inaccuracies by means of musical grammar and syntax, conventionally known as harmony and counterpoint. These branches of the art of Music can be learnt without any reference to sound, as the principles of a foreign language can be acquired without regard for the actual pronunciation of the words. In Music, this "dogmatic composition" as it may be called, can be produced by the application of prescribed rules. It does not indicate the presence of a highly sensitive creative faculty, or even the existence of a delicately responsive ear; it depends upon the application of an eye-test rather than an ear-test, and the composition proceeds by a series of operations which ultimately may be governed by the appearance, not by the sound, of what is written. Thus an exercise in strict counterpoint may be divorced from mental audition, so that it is not "music" so much as a technical problem worked out according to conventional practice.[1]

The hearing of a tune "in the head" is associated with suppressed articulation, but with the composer it is something more.

By means of actual and complete articulation only one audible sound can be produced at a time, but the composer, when recalling or thinking of a musical phrase, does not concentrate his attention only upon the succession of sounds: he makes an effort to hear simultaneously a number of sounds. Hence it is possible that he may be exercising his muscular memory by applying it to his larynx in the attempt to reproduce two or more concurrent sounds. In his case it would appear that the suppressed articulations are not single and successive, but multiple and simultaneous. Obviously a very large range of the sounds that he hears mentally will be outside the limits of his vocal powers, and with cultivation they will follow one another in such rapid succession that the muscular act is eliminated. Here memory and the collateral processes come into play.

3. *Pitch or Tonal Memory.*

Closely related to suppressed articulation is the

[1] "Before his time the *eye* was made the sovereign judge of music, but Scarlatti swore allegiance only to the ear." Burney: *The Present State of Music in Germany, etc.* Second edition, London, 1775, vol. i. p. 253, *n.*

sense of pitch. This may be defined as the faculty of assigning any note, whether sounded or thought, to its exact position in the scale. It is sometimes spoken of as "absolute" pitch, and those who possess it are disposed to connect it with a hypersensitiveness of the auditory apparatus, and to regard it as a rare and mysterious endowment.

The standard of pitch is a convention arrived at after numberless rough and ready experiments, and it would be interesting to investigate our present acceptance of this standard, and to see whether there is any connection between the physiological reaction and the physical nature of sound vibrations.

For a long time pitch was indeterminate, and showed wide extremes. In his translation of *The Sensations of Tone*, by Helmholtz, A. J. Ellis gives the results of his own researches in the form of elaborate tables.[1] From the seventeenth to the nineteenth centuries the divergences were extraordinary, amounting over all to an interval of about a fifth or a minor sixth, and many an organist in older days must have been sorely perplexed by the tuning of a strange instrument when some familiar composition sounded to him higher or lower than the key in which he was accustomed to hear it on his own organ.

The determining of pitch depends on nothing else

[1] p. 493 *et seq*, 3rd ed., 1895.

than practice and habit combined with intelligence. Some musicians possess it acutely, others scarcely at all. A musician may think for a moment before he recognizes the note and almost invariably begins by singing it to himself. He articulates it in silence, and identifies it by associating it with the muscular effort of his larynx necessary to satisfy his ear—by exercising his muscular memory. He may also find it by association, obtaining his bearings by thinking of a familiar piece of music in a given key, but this does not eliminate suppressed articulation, which may be eventually an unconscious act.

The process becomes instantaneous and automatic by training. To orchestral conductors the sense of pitch is indispensable, for by its means they are able to detect without apparent thought a single wrong note played in the midst of what often sounds at rehearsal an incoherent noise. Some composers, who in ordinary circumstances have to think for a moment in determining the pitch of a given note, have their sense intensified by the concentration necessary while conducting, and intuitively correct errors and slips as readily as they would a mistake in speech.

Singers who are accustomed to practise to the accompaniment of a pianoforte tuned to normal pitch, are conscious of any variation from this tuning, and before uttering a sound they feel an unusual tension or relaxation in their larynx. This is experienced by others who are not musicians. Dauriac,[1] who states that he has no voice and can scarcely sing a note in tune, asserts that he has never undergone an act of "*parole intérieure*" without feeling slight pressure or tension, which he locates either in the larynx or its adjoining parts.

What some musicians call "absolute" pitch does not seem to have been clearly defined. It appears to be applicable to a condition in which the ear is hypersensitive to a fixed standard of tuning, and rejects as false in intonation all other sounds which do not coincide with it. Those who play stringed instruments use the pure scale, and develop a sense of pitch which accords with the special character and technique of these instruments. Hence it is that many people, habituated to the tempered scale, have difficulty in convincing themselves that a string quartet is being played "in tune." As the fingering of the fiddle family admits of minute shades of difference, an apparent uncertainty of intonation is perceptible when one stands close beside the violins in a large orchestra, but this disappears at a little distance off, where the various tones of the full body of instruments coalesce.[2]

[1] Dauriac; *Essai sur l'Esprit Musical*, Paris, 1904, p. 77.

[2] See Forsyth, *Orchestration*, p. 378: Macmillan and Stainer & Bell, London, 1914. Also Stanford, *Musical Composition*, p. 114: the same publishers, 1911.

In the instance of the violinist there also must be taken into account the possibility of his muscular memory influencing his intonation, but apart from this, and over and above the "laryngeal test" of pitch, there is, of course, a more intricate and ultimate verification in the brain itself. Here the process will be similar to other mental acts connected with recognition.

4. *Inhibition.*

It has already been said that we cannot at will cut ourselves off from sound. In states of mental abstraction or preoccupation we unconsciously disconnect our auditory apparatus from the perceptive centres through whose co-operation we become aware of sound. Thus inhibition implies attention: they are co-existent. This automatic faculty of inhibition comes into action when one mental process is attacked by another of weaker power, involving a different kind of perception. When the attention is concentrated upon one purpose, sounds, which in periods of mental relaxation might prove violently disturbing, may pass unnoticed.

This suspension of the act of hearing, though it cannot be brought directly under the will, can be controlled to a limited extent, as will be pointed out later when the analysis of orchestral music is discussed.[1]

[1] See p. 113.

The composer, to whom silence or a condition of soundlessness is essential in his work, is particularly disconcerted by "music." A piano next door, street "music" of all kinds, react upon his brain and interrupt the continuity of his thought by producing a disturbance of the ether which physically impinges upon his auditory apparatus, and collides with the studied and orderly adjustment of his mind. These forms of sound are destructive to thought in sound. It is extremely difficult to write down a musical phrase while other music is being performed. The perceptive centres are so acutely stimulated by the external music that the mind cannot "short-circuit" them so as to concentrate itself upon the internal musical phrase. Here the two processes—the perception of external sound and the effort to distinguish internal sound—are parts of the same mental mechanism, but as the mind has greater experience of external than of internal impressions, the stronger power prevails. It is obvious that a technical exercise, demanding of the eye almost as much as of the ear, can be written much more easily during music than composition of an original kind, just as a journalist can work in the midst of conversation which would be distracting to others while writing a letter.

On the other hand music may have an anæsthetic effect and lead the mind into trains of thought unconnected with it. When the faculties are absorbed by ideas remote from music we may hear but we do not listen. The impact of waves of sound and their ultimate distribution over the complex mechanism of the inner ear may produce no mental reaction when the attention is riveted upon other matters.

Inhibition is often strongest while music is being listened to. At public performances the attention is primarily visual and not auditory. The listener may be engrossed in the conductor's gestures, in the "action" of the pianist or violinist, in the host of lesser occurrences on the platform during an orchestral concert, and unless his attention is under control, his mind may wander and drift into other currents. Many people, when describing a concert, begin with what they saw, and this is frequently the most lasting impression. In opera a large portion of the music may escape the ear while there is much movement on the stage. In these cases the auditory perception is the "weaker power," yielding to the visual which is more highly stimulated.

Again there are individuals who, while unable to discriminate between one kind of music and another, find in orchestral music an agreeable influence, and go to concerts in order to work out some train of thought.

Here as before the auditory apparatus ceases to transmit impressions, being inhibited by the stronger power, namely, a group of centres other than auditory and in a more active state.

When the attention is directed wholly to the music there is a suspension of all the perceptive centres not immediately engaged, but beyond this there is an inhibitory control over the auditory apparatus itself, and this may be automatic or voluntary, and at the same time dependent on the acuteness and responsiveness of the listener's musical faculty.

The automatic character is shown in the power of selection with which the ear of the mind is endowed. It is a fundamental law in physics that when a note is struck on a piano, for example, a series of other notes, bearing definite relations to it, is liberated, and these notes are perceptible by those who have trained themselves or have fixed their attention specially to discern them. Were it not for this automatic inhibitory power, music would be an unbearable and detestable noise, and were every partial tone of a generator, particularly in the modern orchestra, to be heard in equal strength, it would demand of the listener exceptional powers of discrimination and analysis to grasp even the outline of the music. In the absence of this form of inhibition sound would be as perturbing as light would be were we living under the influence of a gigantic prism which compelled us to see the world only in the hues of the spectrum.[1]

[1] Perhaps we actually "see" it thus, and our perception of "white" light may be due to the reintegrating power of the rods and cones of the retina.

Many of these partial tones are outside the known range of the human ear, but as they exist as physical facts, and resolve into waves of stronger or weaker impact, all of them must reach us, and the non-perception of them seems to be due to some selective power of the inner ear analogous to the faculty, mentioned in the case of the eye, of suppressing the secondary, the confusing, the unessential image.[1]

In the orchestra the influence of these partial tones has yet to be studied. We are aware, indeed, that light can be disintegrated with the colours of the spectrum as the result. These colours, likewise, can be fused so as to produce white light. The myriad sounds of music may be waves of infinite length proceeding from one tone, but broken up and dispersed through the intervention of a yet to be discovered medium. Thus all sounds may arise from one, and in a great city, after midnight, there still persists to the watchful ear a tone into which casual noises seem to merge.

It is no wide flight of fancy to conjecture that as colour is the dispersion of solar light, and as the spectrum can be recomposed so as to produce white light, sound may be the disintegration of one tone reverberating throughout the universe.

[1] In our present state of knowledge we are not aware of a condition of sound analogous to that of complementary colours in vision.

In its voluntary form inhibition is developed in the musician in close association with analysis. It exists as the result of fixing the attention upon a series of sounds, and varies in intensity in individuals. The simplest operation is that of following the voice part or solo part of a song or instrumental composition with pianoforte accompaniment. First, the tune, whether in the treble or the bass, impresses the mind as being the most homogeneous component of the musical structure, and then the bass upon which it is founded. In seeking for these, the ear suppresses the less important elements, such as subsidiary themes or figures of accompaniment. The musician is conscious of what goes correctly with the melody, and when this is of a straightforward character, he is frequently able not only to complete the phrase mentally before it is actually played, but also to anticipate the bass notes. This is due to the fact that simple tunes have sequences of notes in common at certain points, and many have a strong family resemblance. The perception of the bass comes within the musician's ear-training and proceeds according to established laws: he can discriminate and feel in his own mind alternative versions which might have been used with advantage.

In music of a more elaborate kind, such as sonatas, string quartets and the like, the mind selects the principal "members" of the structure, and eliminates by inhibition, or sets aside for future study, the less prominent but none the less essential contents of the fabric of sound. Short of composing a string quartet there can be no severer test of musicianship than understanding one. Three members of the fiddle family, each with a definite personality, seem to act in antagonism towards one another in order to attain to sublime unity.

The subject and counter-subject of a fugue are recognized and stand out from the rest of the pattern which the ear does not listen to in following them. In these instances the inhibitory power is dependent upon the stage of the musician's development, long practice being necessary in order to gain the facility of isolating a theme from its surroundings. This power is found in its most highly organized form in the act of detaching from the web of orchestral music the part played by some instrument of markedly characteristic timbre, such as the cello or horn, and apparently is a late acquisition. It demands intense concentration as well as exceptional powers of inhibition to confine the ear to one timbre out of many and to exclude all the other sounds. Some musicians cannot sustain the effort for more than three or four bars, the body of sound breaking down their mental resistance so that they lose the thread of the single instrument. With music that is familiar, especially when passages are expected and awaited, the effort of exclusion is less forced, for memory assists, but from the nature of orchestral music, in which every bar has its points of interest, the mind is easily carried away from detail, and impressed by the whole content of the volume of sound.

When the design is simple, as in music of an older style, inhibition is not exercised to any great extent. The pattern is familiar, and whether the music is new to us or not, we have been trained to understand it by having heard other works of a similar kind.

In modern music, in which the design is intricate, it is extremely difficult, as has just been pointed out, to grasp more than a broad idea when we hear it for the first time. On further performances, however, we are able to select important elements in the structure, aided by the unconscious recollection of the earlier experience.

The ear of the mind, then, seizes the essentials, and is deaf to subordinate details. With training it can concentrate itself upon subsidiary constituents, inhibiting the rest of the sound. The educated ear is able to comprehend and identify a number of separate and apparently antagonistic parts which are being played simultaneously, the selection and the inhibition implied in the process being synchronous acts of volition.

5. *Memory.*

From the foregoing sections it will be evident that memory enters into every mental act of the musician, and displays itself in manifold forms. The singer of opera has to remember rôles of immense length, the instrumentalist has his répertoire to master and performs feats of memory without a printed note to fall back upon; the conductor must know his full score practically by heart; the serious composer, apart from knowledge of a technical kind, must be able to keep his attention focussed for long periods upon the details of construction and development which shape themselves rapidly almost in minutes, and yet he may spend days in putting them on paper.

In one respect each is favoured by the nature of his material, for a great deal of music records itself upon the memory automatically. The mind retains, with an exasperating facility, some trivial air not listened to voluntarily, but forced upon it through weakness of the power of inhibition, while it fails too often to bring back the actual words of some large utterance or carefully balanced period.

In everyday conversation we frequently allow our thoughts to drift away from the topic, and occupy ourselves with considering the personality of the speaker or the banality of his remarks. But during audible music, no matter how far removed we may be from conscious listening, or however severe our critical attitude towards the performance, our minds are as wax under the inexorable needle of the recording machine, and many a dreadful tune has triumphed over us through the memory which it has enslaved.

The fact that we are thus the victims of our memory may throw some light in time to come upon the purpose of Music. There is at present no explanation why we remember, often in incongruous circumstances, a musical theme which has thrust itself upon us against our will. Association possibly has a share in the recalling of tunes, but these have little in themselves of the nature of a clue. A musician may make a mental note of an unusual harmony or a striking interval or leap between two notes, and these may assist him in reconstructing a musical phrase, but he has nothing in the way of the idea or a "pivot-word" which helps to recall a verbal sentence.

The catchiness of tunes probably depends to a large extent upon sameness and simplicity of rhythm, as in the waltz, and upon triteness of phrase. The kinds of rhythm used in popular tunes are few, and there are no daring innovations which demand serious thought. The tune itself is remembered probably because it consists of elements which are already in the mind, but some unusual turn of phrase, by stimulating the attention, brings about a reassortment of these elements and completes the record.

This may explain why a "limerick," which adheres to an invariable rhythm, or a scrap of doggerel with its "jingle," is more easily remembered than a couplet weighted with poetic thought or imagery.

The muscular sense in instrumentalists has been alluded to[1] and the conversion of volitional into automatic movements. When a musician at a pianoforte is trying to recall a passage which has escaped him for the moment he does several things. He attempts to hum it: he moves his hands over the keys without striking them: he goes back to a part that he remembers, plays it over, and attempts to run into the forgotten passage. When he finds it it is likely that he will repeat it with some emphasis either with both hands or with each separately. In this proceeding we do not know whether the effort of memory was mental or muscular, or the extent of the one or the other, but from watching the movements of the hands over the keys, we may not be wholly wrong in suggesting that what the brain forgets, the hands may remember.

In some pianists, who read books while practising technical exercises, the muscular movement seems to be independent of conscious thought, and even during a public performance they become oblivious not only of their surroundings but also of their task. By incessantly reproducing dynamic effects of light and

[1] See p. 72.

shade and nuances in general, the muscles acquire a habit, and can simulate the emotion of the music, which the mind, in a state of complete consciousness, endeavoured to convey. This does not apply to many pianists who, never content with the result of their studies, may through a flash of insight "read" a piece of music at a concert in a way that had never before occurred to them.

It is well known that some conductors, when they have an audience behind them, abandon the injunctions which they insisted upon at rehearsal, and allow themselves perfect freedom. To them the rehearsal may have been merely a form of discipline, strictly enforced in order to gain that confidence without which no conductor can play upon his orchestra. What has been called "the inspiration of the moment" may, as will be pointed out later in the chapter,[1] be an act of unconscious memory. The conductor, the instrumentalist, even the singer, have their muscular memory to aid them, but conversely, the mental memory may be so charged with new impulses as to suspend or counteract the muscular "habit" and guide it into unfamiliar actions. Thus a period of conscious work may be succeeded by one of work during unconsciousness.

In a different category is the bewildering accomplishment of those who, without being able to read

[1] See p. 127.

music at all, have taught themselves by ear to play the pianoforte, who learn accompaniments by ear and transpose them without difficulty. This gift is accompanied by the power to extemporize upon given tunes and by a sensitiveness for harmony. Preference also is shown for the keys that contain the largest number of sharps or flats, and the technique, while perhaps it would not satisfy the fastidious, is unquestionably large.

These appear to be instances of a natural predisposition: the muscular aptitude is almost an idiosyncrasy. That such a condition exists is shown by the fact that composers who have not undergone systematic training in pianoforte technique, sometimes play with ease passages in their own compositions which the pure pianist finds awkward.

They develop a technique of their own, however unorthodox it may be, and their hands cultivate an idiom (as it were) which is foreign to the practised pianist. Hence the expression that such and such a work is not written "pianistically."

Extempore playing has just been mentioned. This may be described as the faculty of thinking in terms of music through the medium of a keyed instrument. In *Grove*[1] it is defined as "The art of playing without premeditation, the conception of the music and its rendering being simultaneous." This, how-

[1] Vol. i. p. 798.

ever, must be accepted only in a popular sense, for improvisation depends upon the fact that the conception and the rendering are not, and cannot be simultaneous. In improvising the performer may invent his own theme; the composer in the act of composition frequently improvises while thinking out the development of his ideas. In instances in which improvisation is prescribed as a test of musicianship, the performer is supplied with a theme as the basis of his inventiveness. Frequently one is chosen upon which a fugue can be constructed, and the performer must have an unlimited command of the devices which are employed in this form of composition.

In an exercise of this nature he must decide rapidly the lines upon which he intends to proceed, and as the conception unfolds itself in his mind, he must always be thinking some little way in advance of the bar that he is actually playing, and even be developing mentally a later section complete in itself. The effort of concentration is so great that while he is verifying with his hands one musical thought, he is mentally determining a series of thoughts that are to follow the one that is being played.

What he hears as an external sound is stimulating his mind to the conception of further sounds. In this form of creative thought the material that he is playing at one moment is not identical with the material that is being shaped in his mind at the same moment, and they may not be related to one another except as parts of the whole conception.

We may compare the process with the delivery of an extempore speech. During this, the speaker's mind is rapidly making a note of the points that are to be touched upon, the muscles of the organ of speech acting in relation to the utterance as the muscles of the hands do in the musical act.

The musical mind is capable of rapid and continuous thought associated with muscular co-ordination, and the manual act appears to be reflex, the result of indescribably brief acts of memory.

Many improvisations appear to depend on the performer's memory, and strictly speaking are not unpremeditated, for he may interpolate familiar passages derived from past experience in order to gain time for considering fresh developments of his theme. A fact to be noted is that the mind does not demand of the hands work that it cannot perform, and the improviser who is not a brilliant pianist keeps within his limitations. This is characteristic of the performer who plays entirely by ear. If a number of his improvisations are listened to attentively, it will be found that they break loose somewhere, after the first effort of concentration has spent itself, and drift into passages based upon two or three pianistic formulæ.[1]

[1] An instance of this may be given from my own experience. I was stopping at an hotel in the country and on the evening of

Reference has been made to the constructive act of the composer and to his being compelled to retain in his mind innumerable details for long stretches of time. The purely physical conditions of his work develop his memory to an enormous extent, for in the act of recording his ideas his imagination often is far ahead of the notes that he is writing at the moment, and it may be weeks before he overtakes it. The analysis of a single bar in a full score brings to light the host of technicalities which the composer has to command. The laying out of the harmony so that the instruments will balance one another and fuse into sound; the knowledge of their limitations as to compass, systems of fingering and effectiveness of register; the perception of their timbre; the assigning of the "high lights" to this group, of the "background" to that,—these must be under his control so absolutely that he can dispose them without apparent thought.

In addition, he must have the faculty of analyzing, in terms of the orchestra, sounds heard mentally. With practice he may arrive at a rule-of-thumb procedure in the orchestration of some straightforward sections, but the serious composer is not

my arrival I heard the sound of a piano. I was certain not only of an improvisation, but also of the identity of the pianist. He was an ear-taught extempore player, a former colleague whom I had not met for fifteen years.

content with such a method, and prefers to write what he himself hears, not what others think he ought to hear.

It will be evident that this form of analytical memory is to be acquired only by experience and deep efforts of concentration. Some composers possess it so acutely that they do not find it necessary to reconsider passages after having heard them once or twice; others, on hearing one of their orchestral works for the first time, are surprised that it sounds totally different from what they expected, and in their uncertainty of what sounds they wish, are constantly altering the scoring. Impatience or haste may be the cause of this, but it is more likely that they have disregarded the warning that what looks well on paper does not always sound well, and have trusted to the eye rather than to the inner ear.

These are instances of specific acts which concern technique. But beyond them there is the wide domain of composition itself. Into this we cannot enter far, for we are speedily checked by the unknowable: the mystery of creative thought cannot be explored. There is, however, an aspect which can be considered, and that is the part that unconscious memory plays in Music. By this is meant the exercising of the memory in the effort of composition while the composer is under the impression that his mind is occupied with new material. Instances are at hand on all sides of composers having unconsciously reproduced themes occurring in well-known works, and nothing so gladdens the heart of those who, in Dauriac's phrase,[1] are "afflicted with the monomania for resemblances." These need not distract us; the composer who is jealous for his work is the last deliberately to fall back upon the ideas of others.

Unconscious memory may be more strictly defined as the process by which the composer reproduces his own themes, but transformed in such a way that he does not at first perceive any resemblance. When he is possessed by a strong and vital conception in music, no matter how far he may abstract himself from it, it may be predominant in his subsequent thoughts, entering intimately into association with the germinal theme upon which his elaboration is founded.

From the point of view of construction music has been carried many stages beyond the primitive statement of theme that sufficed in its younger days. It is enough to place a page of an early symphony beside a modern work in order to be convinced that, apart from æsthetics (which we are not considering) something has happened. It is as if we were comparing a piece of mummy-wrapping with a panel of Flemish tapestry. Up to our own day, in the larger forms of music, it was the practice to announce the principal themes and to repeat them in their

[1] Dauriac: *op. cit.* p. 176.

entirety before the development was entered upon. Frequently this "development" was nothing else than a good deal of irresponsible splashing about in the orchestra without much reference to the subject-matter. Nowadays development has been carried much further, and instead of clearly defined sections, such as were employed in the classic "first-and-second-subject" plan, the effort is made to make the discourse more wide and rhetorical. In this the thematic basis of the movement frequently seems to have been forgotten, as if the composer had allowed himself to be carried away by the rush of ideas. In some instances constructive effort may be deliberate, but if we investigate the conditions under which certain compositions were written, we often find that although the composer seems to have gone so far beyond his primary idea as to have lost sight of it, the apparently irrelevant matter is nevertheless closely related to it. It may, indeed, pass undiscovered by the composer himself till his attention is called to its actual presence in material which he imagined was wholly unconnected with it.

In such cases the composer is riveted to the primary idea, and is unconsciously elaborating it, although it may appear to have passed out of his mind.

This unconscious use and persistence of a theme may be discovered in a group of works upon which a composer is engaged. An example may be found in another art, where a portrait painter, struck by one type of face, reproduces some of its characteristics in every other that he paints until the potency of that type is exhausted. It is not difficult, in a case that has come under my observation, to ascribe to this subtle influence a series of portraits, all vastly different in design and in the personality of the sitters, as indicating definite periods in the artist's career.

In a chapter headed "Mathematical Discovery," Henri Poincaré[1] gives a close analysis of the processes by which some mathematical problems and their solutions occurred to him. If "Music" is substituted for "Mathematics," the description is a clear one, in my own experience at least, of the evolution of musical ideas. After giving a description of how some of his own discoveries were made, he continues: "Often when a man is working at a difficult question, he accomplishes nothing the first time he sets to work. Then he takes more or less of a rest, and sits down again at his table. During the first half-hour he still finds nothing, and then at once the decisive idea presents itself to his mind. We might say that the conscious work proved more fruitful because it was interrupted, and the rest restored force and freshness to the mind. But it is more probable that the rest was occupied with unconscious work, and that the

[1] Henri Poincaré: *Science and Method*, translated by Francis Maitland. London: 1914, pp. 46-53.

result of this work came during a period of conscious work, but independently of that work, which at most only performs the unlocking process, as if it were the spur that excited into conscious form the results already acquired during the rest, which till then remained unconscious."

"Regarding the conditions of this unconscious work, it is not possible, or in any case not fruitful, unless it is first preceded by a period of conscious work." He speaks of "days of voluntary effort which appeared absolutely fruitless. . . . These efforts, however, were not as barren as one thought; they set the unconscious machine in motion, and without them it would not have worked at all."

In the composer Music exists as a form of thought, and his musical sense is always in a state of activity, whether his attention as regards Music is concentrated or apparently suspended. We know that the musical memory records, frequently against our will, a kind of Music that we would be only too glad to exclude from our minds if we had the power. We become suddenly conscious of a tune, but are unable to trace the route by which it sprang into our memory: we find ourselves in possession of something, without a sign of how we acquired it. Are we warranted in assuming that there is within us an indefinable agency, ever awake? Is there in man's system a process yet to be defined which continues to act in periods of unconsciousness, as the heart, the lungs and other organs? Is it possible that thought and memory in themselves may be analogous to secretions, discharging their functions during states of unconsciousness?

These are questions confronting the investigator who is abroad not to invent new problems so much as to discover solutions for the old.

Everyone who turns his thoughts and his hand seriously to the Art of Music must acknowledge to himself that however minutely he may scrutinize the workings of his own mind, however accurately he may mark off and record the incidental occurrences of his senses, he is powerless to gauge the means that he employs. Small or great as he may be, of wide reading or profoundly ignorant, there still remains the unexplained and inexplicable.

Nowadays all are alert for discovery, and the unknown has become a commonplace. Deliberately and without loss of time camps are pitched where man never trod. But the realm of Music is still unexplored. Captains arise and victories are theirs: their path is strewn with the wreckage of those who knew how to serve but were found wanting in command. But those who minister to this art, which has crept so surely into the needs of man, go forth on their errand rejoicing, for the unravelling is not for them, but the clear and whole vision.

CHAPTER VII

HEREDITY

In the present study it is not for us to dogmatize upon questions which are absorbing the attention of skilled observers, but rather to suggest the minute scrutiny of every mental phase connected with Music as a creative and interpretative art.

Elsewhere[1] I considered, somewhat discursively perhaps, the general bearings of the theory of Heredity, and ventured to suggest that in the special case of Music, an art which cannot be practised in silence, environment might have a definite influence upon the child that grew up in musical surroundings, and that what was called Heredity might be in many instances Continuity of Vocation, as I termed it.

The charge of going over old ground must be risked here, for the subject comes within the scope of our inquiry.

[1] See *The Threshold of Music*, ch. xiii., Heredity and Environment.

Some general observations may be offered at the outset. It is unlikely that many now hold to the theory that mental characteristics can be transmitted to the offspring. The son of a peer inherits his father's title and lands : the law sees to that : but it does not follow that he inherits his abilities or his vices. These are the result of his environment. The son of a scientific man does not inherit his father's university degrees or honours. The law sees to that also. Art, science, knowledge, have no charters, no muniments : blood-pedigree they may cherish with pride, but they cannot transmit brain-pedigree.

The son of a man who has distinguished himself in science is brought up in surroundings which stimulate him to cultivate a close habit of thought. He lives in a special "atmosphere": his mind is being educated without his being aware that any significant process is at work. At school and at the university he is marked because of his father's attainments: he comes in contact with men familiar with his father's career: he is impressed by his father's influence over men of the world: he aspires to be like him, and in turn to wield some of that influence. On the strength of his own endeavours and also through the name he bears he obtains an appointment in which he cannot go far astray, and continues his father's work in a field which has been carefully prepared for him.

This holds good in other professions, particularly

in the Services and in Law: in Medicine the son often steps into his father's "good-will." But it is equally true that in many instances the son does not reach his father's eminence, not because of any mental incompetence, but because the work prescribed for him does not afford a scope for individual expansion. Who knows how far the popular idea of "heredity" may have been the means of sterilizing an original thinker? He may have been thrust into the paternal groove through family tradition, through the counsels of his elders, through immediate necessities for a livelihood; and many a mind, conscious of its own freedom, but scarcely realizing its extent, may have been delivered into bondage and sacrificed to the fetish of heredity.

Galton made out a case in his famous work, *Hereditary Genius*,[1] but one cannot overlook the possibility of special pleading, for he was a member of a family distinguished in science. He says indeed in regard to that family: "There is a strong element of individuality in the different members of the race which is adverse to traditional influence." This seems to indicate that while he laid stress upon family tendencies, he asserted the presence of individuality, and so long as "heredity" did not dispossess him of his claim to be an original investigator, he was prepared

[1] Galton, *Hereditary Genius*, 2nd edition, 1892, p. 203.

to support it. The sentence reads as if he had the glimmering of a fear lest his own researches might be attributed through his own theory of heredity to the strong scientific bent that existed in the family, and not to personal distinction. No one to-day regards Galton as overshadowed by his relatives—his work has its own value—but in view of the importance which he gives to individual effort it is not a little singular that he made no attempt to break through the traditional influence, if only by the instinct of self-preservation.

Investigators so far have based the case for heredity upon historical evidence. Galton swept everybody of consequence, and many of none, into his net. He adduced his own family and connections, but was prevented "by a sense of decorum"[1] from dealing with the relatives of contemporaries who had not been recognized as public characters. It is to be hoped that his records will be accessible when a discreet period has elapsed, for it is possibly the plodding and less brilliant members of talented families who might supply valuable information.

It is a characteristic of some minds—often a failing—to cultivate the bond of family by pedigree-hunting, and even rascality has a picturesque charm of its own when Time, the Old Master, has toned down the high lights. It is natural to attempt to account for a

[1] Galton: *op. cit.*, p. 3.

distinguishing mental trait in an individual by seeking among his progenitors for one of a similar kind, and the popular idea has grown to such an extent that the belief in heredity has become a superstition.

In the cases which we have to study, however, we have just the same material to investigate that Galton and others had, but it is in the inferences that we must be more guarded. In any inquiry the scientific man would be the first to reject evidence that he had been unable to verify for himself, and in a question like the one before us, dealing as it does with a highly organized mental act, it will not suffice to rely upon bare facts taken from biographical dictionaries, without at the same time considering conditions of life, opportunities, surroundings, and a host of external influences.

The theory of heredity in musicians owes a great deal to the genealogy of the Bach family, perhaps the most conspicuous example in history of a vocation persisting in the members of one family over a lengthened period. Johann Sebastian himself was struck with this continuity of musical ability and drew up the family pedigree.[1]

But when we consider the age in which the Bachs lived (from 1561 till 1845, when the last died, the 24th in the line of musicians), when we consider them thrown back upon themselves for education and

[1] See *The Threshold of Music*, pp. 112-13, 220-23.

society, brought up always in close touch with music, and developing a kind of clanship, we are not surprised that their segregation encouraged the cultivation of one form of art, and one alone. Music in the Bachs was contagious.

If we take into account the surroundings and life of the centuries in which they flourished, we find the conditions specially favourable for self-absorption, but the line became attenuated after Johann Sebastian's death in 1750, and ultimately expired when the affairs of the world impinged upon the family and disturbed its serenity. Music was crowded out.

Convincing as the Bach pedigree appears, it would be impregnable as evidence of heredity had a parallel instance been met with in some other art which could have been pursued in silence, but we have none.

Connected with music there are physical elements to be considered. Whether the child is brought up among musical people or not, he hears music in some form in his daily life, but much more intensely when his parents or brothers or sisters practise music as a profession or recreation. He "picks it up" just as the English child born in India acquires a smattering of Hindustani—just as on many a Highland estate the child whose parents "have no English," that is, who speak only Gaelic, is bi-lingual owing to association with speakers of English in school hours and to practical needs. The English child acquires Hindustani, the Gaelic child acquires English, not by heredity but by environment. And so, nowadays, does every child acquire the power of singing.

There are, further, purely physical reasons for the child of a violinist, following his father's career. He hears music from his cradle: he cannot exclude the sounds of practising: he becomes familiar with the tools of his father's calling. He may excel, or fall far short of, his father's accomplishment, but, given the environment, the stimulus is present. Had he been out of reach of the stimulus it is doubtful whether he would have grown up a musician.

In numbers of families of instrumentalists the vocation has been continued. Many of these, the great bulk, indeed, have not attained sufficient eminence to gain a place in the biographical dictionaries, the only works of reference that lie to our hand. It is therefore possible that the case of an instrumentalist, brought up without the environment, has escaped notice owing to his having passed his life in obscurity. For our purpose it is not a little unfortunate that we have to deal only with those who won some fame, and were discussed by over-partial biographers in search of anything which could illuminate their subject, and we may be accepting many highly-coloured statements as facts.

As distinct from the qualities necessary in the

instrumentalist, the composer's faculty is one that he cannot impart to his son, no matter what the environment is, for he works in silence. The surroundings may be musical and music may be heard incessantly, but the son acquires nothing from the creative effort of his father until it is performed and realized in sound; but then it ceases to be the son's exclusive inheritance.

We now come to examine more particularly the examples other than those of the Bachs, which have been adduced as proof of heredity.

When Galton published his remarkable book, *Hereditary Genius*, in the year 1869, many were in a frame of mind to accept any theory which seemed to be related to or to support the investigations of Charles Darwin and Alfred Russel Wallace, and while in the work to which we will immediately refer there are many examples to be found, illustrating but not confirming its thesis—as, for instance, the purely "caste" profession of Law—the proofs to be derived from Music are slender, showing that the art is still young, and has not had time to accumulate characters in the strength necessary for their transmission.

Here it is not an individual development but one affecting man in large communities and civilizations, and dependent upon the progress of the musical faculty generally.

Galton found so little to say about musicians that we may quote it all.[1]

> The general remarks I made in the last chapter on artists apply with equal force to Musicians. The irregularity of their lives is commonly extreme; the union of a painstaking disposition with the temperament requisite for a good musician is as rare as in poets, and the distractions incident to the public life of a great performer are vastly greater. Hence, although the fact of the inheritance of musical taste is notorious and undeniable, I find it exceedingly difficult to discuss its distribution among families. I also found it impossible to obtain a list of first-class musicians that commanded general approval, of a length suitable for my purposes. There is excessive jealousy in the musical world, fostered no doubt by the dependence of musicians upon public caprice for their professional advancement. Consequently, each school disparages others; individuals do the same, and most biographers are unusually adulatory of their heroes, and unjust to those with whom they compare them. There exists no firmly-established public opinion on the merits of musicians, similar to that which exists in regard to poets and painters, and it is even difficult to find private persons of fair

[1] Galton: *op. cit.*, p. 230.

> musical tastes, who are qualified to give a deliberate and dispassionate selection of the most eminent musicians. . . . I was indebted to a literary and artistic friend in whose judgment I have confidence, for the selection upon which I worked.

The "general remarks"[1] to which Galton refers are these :—

> "The Poets and Artists generally are men of high aspirations, but, for all that, they are a sensuous, erotic race, exceedingly irregular in their way of life. . . . Their talents are usually displayed early in youth, when they are first shaken by the tempestuous passion of love."

In connection with the second quotation, which must be read with the first, we are struck by the fact that in the twenty-three years that intervened between the appearance of the two editions of his book, Galton did not reconsider in the light of his own researches the strictures which he passed upon the Poet, the Artist, and the Musician. His right to speak of some as "extremely irregular in their way of life" is indisputable, but we are surprised that he was content to make the assertion without noticing the volume of light that it shed upon his own difficulties.

In an inquiry that depends almost wholly upon the testimony of others now beyond our reach, the

[1] *Op. cit.*, p. 218.

source of our material must be biographies and dictionaries which record the life-histories of those who made a name for themselves. Men who are "exceedingly irregular" are not the people whose exploits, creditable or the reverse, are chronicled in such works of reference. In the annals of musicians at least, as will be shown later,[1] the standard of living could not have been so debased as Galton suggested, for, as we shall see, the average of life is a good one.

There are instances of wreckage, no doubt, in everybody's experience, but these are not to be counted against Art more than against any other vocation. It used to be asserted that some of the greatest moments in literature were begotten of garlic and bad brandy, and not a few poets have been placed upon probation for immortality whose propensities and failings we know unfortunately too well. But when it is a question of the means for the setting down of ideas, time is all on the side of the man of letters. The divine ictus may hammer a canto into shape over-night, but statues and full-length portraits and symphonies do not leap forth, panoplied, between twilight and dawn. The composer of serious music knows too well that the balance between impression and expression is delicately poised, and he does not tamper with it.

Were Galton alive to-day to estimate the weight

[1] See pp. 183-5.

of his theory in regard to Music in the light of more recent studies and perplexing developments, he would find much to confirm in his longer statement, much, too, to modify or amend. We are not told who the 120 musicians were, "the most original and eminent upon record,"[1] who were selected by Galton's friend. Musical biography in the year 1869 had not been brought to the completeness that it enjoys to-day, and the *Biographie* of Fétis, the largest of the time, was untrustworthy. The cases that Galton adduced are only sixteen in all, giving the ratio of 13.3 per cent., scarcely the overwhelming figure upon which to found any theory. His plea that he "finds it extremely difficult to discuss" the distribution of musical taste among families is quite comprehensible, and it is likely that he had misgivings as to his results when he came to look into the pedigrees.

We now take his proofs.

Allegri's musical relative (with a query) was not a musician, but Correggio the painter.

The Amatis were not musicians, but craftsmen.

Bach and Beethoven are admitted.

Benda's is a valuable pedigree of lesser musicians.

In Bononcini, Dussek, Eichhorn, Gabrielli (more usually Gabrieli), Haydn, Hiller, and Keiser, we find music persisting in two generations.

Mendelssohn's case will be discussed later.[2] The

[1] *Op. cit.*, p. 232. [2] See p. 175.

persistence of musical accomplishment in his family, which provided the environment, must have encouraged him, but it is difficult to see what his sister Fanny's being "also very affectionate" has to do with heredity.

In Meyerbeer the musical heredity seems to have been based on the fact that one of his brothers was an astronomer, and another "a poet of high promise, who died young."

Mozart and Palestrina, whom we do not challenge, complete the list.

Eliminating Allegri, Amati and Meyerbeer, the ratio is reduced to 10.8 per cent., and it is noteworthy that only six of the sixteen, Bach, Beethoven, Haydn, Mendelssohn, Mozart and Palestrina, flourish with us now. But they lived in a musical atmosphere, accidental and external: their surroundings undoubtedly influenced the musical tendencies of their minds, but that is not heredity.

It is in this that confusion has arisen, and it is well to be clear on the point. It may not be of much moment whether the creative musical faculty is inherited or not: imperfect records in the past may have kept out of sight genuine cases of the inheritance of musical ability, though it is scarcely likely that an enthusiastic biographer would have passed over anything that might add lustre to his hero.

But if we accept history, we must admit that there

is no instance of abundant creative talent persisting in any family outside the Bachs. There are examples of interpretative talent having been handed down from father to son through environment and continuity of vocation, but no great composer was the father, or the son, of an equally great composer.

This must not be regarded as an attempt to demolish what has become at its best a cherished tradition, at its worst a superstition. Many a musical family has been, in Galton's phrase, "notorious and undeniable," but this does not solve the problem. Some families produce nothing more than talented people who are unable to break away from their intimate circle; others have contributed several members to the ranks of orchestral players,[1] but, it must be repeated here, the creative is distinct from the interpretative mind.

Heredity is not concerned with the degree of celebrity to which a musician attains, and many indisputably potent "strains" may have been passed by owing to the inability of a family to bring forth a distinguished scion whose work would call attention to the lesser gifts of his kinsmen.

I have already stated the conditions[2] which have

[1] In every country this must be the case. In England members of the same family are frequently met with in the large orchestras.

[2] See p. 136.

to be taken into consideration in the musically-adapted child, and we may now look into historic cases.

The Tables at the end of Chapter VIII. contain a list of composers drawn up for another purpose,[1] but they may be taken as fairly representative. Each name has been verified in the second edition of *Grove*.

We find the following :—

TABLE I. Musicians persisting in three generations or more in the families of

Bach	Gibbons	Philidor	Scarlatti
Couperin	Lully	Piccinni	Weber
Field	Mozart	Purcell	(15 per cent.)

TABLE II. Composers in whose families there were recognized professional musicians of the same, or the preceding or following generations.

Beethoven	Cherubini	W. Lawes	Rossini
Bellini	Dowland	Offenbach	Schubert
Boccherini	Haydn	Palestrina	Sullivan
Brahms	O. di Lasso	Rameau	Sweelinck
Byrd	H. Lawes	(25 per cent.)	

It will be observed that these tables are classified more strictly than Galton's, to whom I have conceded Mendelssohn, who, in spite of the musical tendencies of his family, ought by heredity to have been a banker. It is possible to compile from the dictionaries and biographies other examples of families in which musical ability was found in two or more

[1] See pp. 182, 184.

generations. The present object, however, is to examine the life-histories of a number of composers who were chosen to illustrate historical stages in the development of the Art. Of the others in Tables III. and IV. several are mentioned by *Grove* as having begun their musical instruction at home. These amount to 14 per cent. of the 70, thus leaving the fairly high ratio of 46 per cent. of composers in whose families there are no records of musical tendencies. As it is scarcely likely that the musical ability of the parents would have been overlooked in the documents at hand, we may conclude that any fresh evidence would be negative and thus tend to lower the percentage on the side of heredity.

It is to be noted that the families showing the strongest musical tendency "kept together" more than the others. The twelve Couperins, a striking example overlooked by Galton, retained in the family two appointments for 200 years, an instance of efficiency, with possibly influence to support it.[1]

In regard to what has been said as to discriminating between the creative and interpretative sides of Music, it is right to point out that in the earlier days of the art the composer was a performer as well, and often had to depend entirely upon his instrument for support. An intermediate stage was that reached by

[1] For the pedigree of this family see the end of this chapter.

Berlioz and Wagner, indifferent pianists, who concentrated their attention on composition alone, and did not take part in public performances except as conductors of their own works or of orchestral concerts in general. They might be termed "pure composers," along with Verdi and others who wrote for the stage. Coincident with them was another group of musicians, mainly executants, producing a certain amount of musical compositions, which, however, had no enduring quality.

A third group has been formed to-day, and the younger generation of composers is showing not only a high degree of proficiency in composition, but also a masterly command of an instrument, thus testifying to the further development of the musical faculty. It remains to be seen whether, with the present trend of orchestral music, the dual facility can be equally sustained, or one branch alone cultivated.

In this aspect the utmost care has to be exercised in investigating cases, and it is to the human documents themselves that the scientific man must turn. The composer of our own day is not unintelligent, and though he himself, or his friends, may naturally be disposed to assign the presence of his gift to some parental influence, and thus to call it "inherited," it is for the man of science to apply to his study the same rules that he would insist upon in examining any other human faculty. In the case of Music a mass of "evidence" has been admitted which in any other inquiry would have been rejected at the outset, and this has vitiated the conclusions.

Some researches have already been undertaken in this direction, but the results must be viewed strictly in relation to the object of the investigation. Although the article,[1] to which reference will be made presently, deals, as its title indicates, with a theory of heredity which is primarily concerned with physical characters in plants and animals, it discusses certain physical features in man, mainly pigmentation, but also, strange to say, musical temperament. We must distinguish between the artistic musical faculty and the ability to sing, but it must be pointed out that of the eleven sections in Hurst's essay ten deal with characters over which the individual has no control, such as eye-colour, hair-colour, skin-colour in "white" races, while musical temperament is prefaced by the following hasty generalizations:

"That certain individuals have a natural disposition for Music, while others have not, is evident to the most casual observer."

This we do not dispute, but the next sentence runs:

"That this natural disposition or temperament is innate and hereditary there can be little doubt.

[1] C. C. Hurst: "Mendelian Heredity in Man," *Eugenics Review*, vol. iv., No. 1, April, 1912, pp. 20-21.

Musical associations and careful training can, of course, do much in enriching the musical qualities in an individual of a musical disposition, but in the absence of the musical temperament these outer stimuli are practically powerless."

It is evident that Hurst does not attach the same meaning to "musical heredity" as Galton has done, for the cases which we have just been considering are those of ripe musicians. Hurst, on the other hand, bases his thesis on observations made among children of the ages of from two to six years, the only test of their "musical temperament" being their natural ability to sing or learn a tune, a very different thing from the faculty which we are studying.

In addition to the sense in which the word "heredity" is used there is a further question of terminology, for the musician attaches two meanings to "musical temperament." In acoustics it refers to the division of the scale: but more popularly the musician understands by it a mental condition, usually of adult life but also to be found in the young, indicating a varying degree of sensitiveness to music in its higher forms. It is a phrase which, like "artistic temperament,"[1] is frequently misused, and, seeing that Hurst's investigations apply to an extremely limited field in the vast domain of Music, we should be better off if we had an expression to describe "tone-percep-

[1] See p. 191.

tion" as distinct from the trained musician's faculty. There is manifestly a wide gap between the musical temperament of a child of six years, and the musically artistic temperament of an adult of twenty. Music to the educated man implies a complex mental endowment which the child of six does not as a rule possess. The rare technical ability which was referred to in Chapter V is in a totally different category.

By classing this "musical temperament" with other characters purely physical, Hurst possibly implies that the child's earliest song is also physical. Song primarily is a muscular effort; a gesture, in fact. The child cries before he sings, and sings before he speaks. His cry is the first human utterance that is common to, and understood by, mankind all the world over. The last is the death-wail. Between these extremes speech and language intervene to complicate life from the incoming to the outgoing. The tongue that the child speaks is the tongue of his parents; the song that he sings is the song of his parents, and the nature of the tongue and the song are determined by latitude and longitude, and by nothing else.

A theory of heredity in poetry or oratory is not based on the fact that the child had literate parents. We do not detect the artistic faculty in children through their being addicted to the habit of defacing with a pencil any flat surface, preferably the wall of a public building.

In the newly-born child there is little that we actually can see that is inherent. He is a parasite until he is weaned. In his earlier months he is busier than at any other period of his life, for he has everything to learn ; but no one asserts that he has the makings of a great composer because he composes and improvises for himself his own songs. Providence takes care that this propensity, at least, becomes attenuated.

While Hurst's inquiries may serve to demonstrate Mendel's Law—and this is not disputed here—they do not and cannot throw any light upon the special question whether the capacity for Music as an art is transmitted or not. It is not outside the bounds of possibility that that Law may yet be applied to mental processes and tendencies, for Science has a way of her own for dealing with negations, but although the results which we are now considering may have no bearing upon the faculty for Music as we understand it, there is something to be gained from a study of the presence of the power to sing.

Let us go to history. If the infant's singing before the age of six had anything whatever to do with "Music," we should have had great musical works of art down the ages. But we have none till Palestrina's time. We assume that the singing voice, like the speaking voice, has been man's possession for centuries, and the most ancient examples of recorded music testify to the existence of song. But the heritage of song is not the inheritance of a highly organized faculty for composing music.

Hurst says, "Musical children as they grow up begin to harmonize naturally, putting in their own parts without any tuition."[1] But this is quite a recent faculty of civilized man, at the most two centuries old. Contemporary records, if they are to be trusted, demonstrate that the musicians of the twelfth and thirteenth centuries were unable to do what the child to-day does automatically. The sculptors in that period were literal enough: they did not hesitate to carve what they saw. But if Music had been as highly organized as Sculpture, there was nothing in its nature to prevent men from writing down what they heard and sang. If we are to believe that they sang naturally in harmony, as the child does now, the mystery is that they did not preserve the fact in their written music. We have to go to documents for our knowledge of the music of past times, but if the child of the dark ages sang as we sing as children, it is of immense significance that no proofs remain. Whatever view we may take of the present condition of the musical faculty in civilized man—whether it is a new one that has come into existence in the last few

[1] See *The Threshold of Music*, p. 71, "The instinctive reproduction by an unskilled singer of certain conventional musical phrases which took centuries of theorizing to formulate shows what a change has taken place in the average mind."

hundred years or one that was latent—whether it has attained to a degree of extreme sensitiveness in the past century, or we ourselves have undergone a definite and rapid change in actual perception—we must take account of the host of conditions under which it has been evolved.

In researches into the mental endowment of musicians, the special characters of Music must be kept in view. Hitherto the distinction has not been made between the development of the song-voice and the musical gift. The one may not reveal itself in early childhood: the other may show signs of maturity too soon: each may progress slowly. Again, there has been a tendency to accept as "musical" those who have song and little else—*vox et praeterea nihil.* This is misleading. Hurst, for instance, says, "There seems also to be a striking difference between musical and non-musical people in the nature of their ordinary speaking voice, the musical individual speaks naturally in melodious tones, the voice rising and falling with correct intervals, while the non-musical individual speaks naturally in monotones without a trace of melody. So far, only one case has been observed by the writer where a non-musical individual has a melodious speaking voice, and not a single case where a musical individual has a monotonous voice."

Once more we are perplexed by terminology, but even with Hurst's restricted use of the word "musical," his contention is purely personal, for it is well known among musicians that one particularly unmusical kind of voice is named *la voix du compositeur*, the voice, in fact, of the man who is endowed with the highest form of the musical faculty. Further, many who are afflicted with stammer have pleasant singing voices. Burney wrote of Gluck's singing that "he so well compensated for the want of voice that it was a defect which was soon entirely forgotten."[1] We are told[2] that in his early days of hardship in Paris, Wagner attempted to secure an engagement in the chorus of a small boulevard theatre, but was rejected on account of his lack of voice. One of the most distinguished of modern French composers says that his voice is not absolutely in tune, and that he has to make an intellectual effort before singing certain notes.[3]

The melodiousness of the speaking voice has no connection with music: it depends on the anatomical formation of the larynx, and is primarily muscular.[4]

[1] Burney, *op. cit.*, vol. i. p. 264.

[2] Lavignac, *The Music Dramas of Richard Wagner* (Lond. 1898), p. 27.

[3] Vincent d'Indy, *Lettre inédite*, 1905, quoted by Lalo, *Esquisse d'une Esthétique musicale scientifique* (Paris, 1908), p. 218, *n.*

[4] Many a boy's melodious treble, through anatomical changes when the voice breaks, becomes an uncertain tenor or a disagreeable bass.

No power on earth can coerce a larynx anatomically unfitted for song into an organ that is fitted for it. Laborious training and intelligence may minimize defects, and practice may ultimately conceal a rasping note, but a melodious speaking voice is no more characteristic of the musician than are long slender fingers typical of the artist. A moment's thought of the work that the sculptor, the painter or the pianist has to perform with his hands would speedily dispel that view. The development of the *lumbricales*, so essential for violin or piano playing, increases the breadth of the hands and puts an end to their grace. But the grace of the mind remains.

Owing to the impossibility of bringing up a child in surroundings which are sound-proof, the influence of environment cannot be excluded in a study of the application of Mendel's Law to tone-perception. The Law is engrossing in this, that man has experimented upon forms of life lower than his own, and has been able to observe and control varieties of activity which grow rapidly to maturity, and, so far as we know, take no thought for the morrow. But for man there is no fixed law of evolution, and when the investigator compares his own kindred, endowed with special attributes and special powers of attraction and selection, with the behaviour of flowers and butterflies under certain conditions, he overlooks one element in his supremacy, and that is the mind. In man's economy Mendel's Law is of inestimable value in determining the best means for co-ordinating the forms of life upon which he depends for his daily support and sustenance. So far it has accounted for purely physical anomalies in man, and from the point of view of eugenics its effect will be far-reaching and revolutionary, but, in questions of the faculties, the race is not yet ready, and will not be until physical is placed before mental development.

When a child's tone-perception is under observation, much attention should be paid to his surroundings, for a tune-phrase is learnt and remembered with far less effort than a word-phrase. The "natural disposition for music" would be unassailable had Hurst brought forward an instance of a child less than three years of age singing, note for note, his father's song, but even this would not eliminate environment and establish heredity.[1]

Whatever lies before us in the path of evolution, it is undoubted that civilized man is infinitely more predisposed to Music now than he was only a short time ago in the world's history, and this modification of his mental environment may hasten the develop-

[1] My earliest recollection is of a concert to which I was taken at the unreasonable age of two and a half years. My father had been singing a solo, and when I was being carried out in the nurse's arms at the end, I sang what he had sung, and the words were Latin.

ment of the faculties which enlarge and expand in favourable surroundings. The cultivation of the art of Music is now an accepted factor in our modern life, but generations must pass before any assertion can be made that the creative gift, or even the power of tone-perception, is innate. We cannot voluntarily cut ourselves off from all sound, although under certain conditions, demanding the exercise of the will, or during deep concentration, the act of hearing may be suspended. This cannot take place in the child, for when there is music in the household he is not able to escape from it, and while we do not know the character and extent of his auditory impressions, we note in his articulations an attempt to imitate what he hears. We saw[1] that the ear must be conscious of external sounds before mental sounds can be realized. It would be absurd to say that the composer's highly organized faculty is also present in the child; but whether the child eventually becomes a musician or gets little beyond singing snatches of tune, his earliest appreciation of musical sounds depends on what he hears in his surroundings. He is being unconsciously educated, and his undeveloped larynx is being shaped, as his limbs are, ultimately to fulfil their functions in his physical economy.

The question of Mendelism, however, presents great difficulties owing to the impossibility of isolat-

[1] See p. 97.

ing and "insulating" the child from birth. The presence of what Hurst[1] calls the musical sense could be proved as innate only by experiments carried out under conditions so stringent that a habeas corpus writ would follow as a matter of course. In Music we unquestionably are dealing with a faculty which even at birth can be brought under external influences and the control of others, but this is a human factor very different from pigmentation.

The Ethiopian cannot change his skin, but one of his race, in the twentieth century, won world-wide fame with his music.

[1] C. C. Hurst, "Mendel's Law of Heredity and its Application to Man: *Trans. Leicester Literary and Philosophical Society*, vol. xii. pt. 1, January, 1908.

THE COUPERIN PEDIGREE

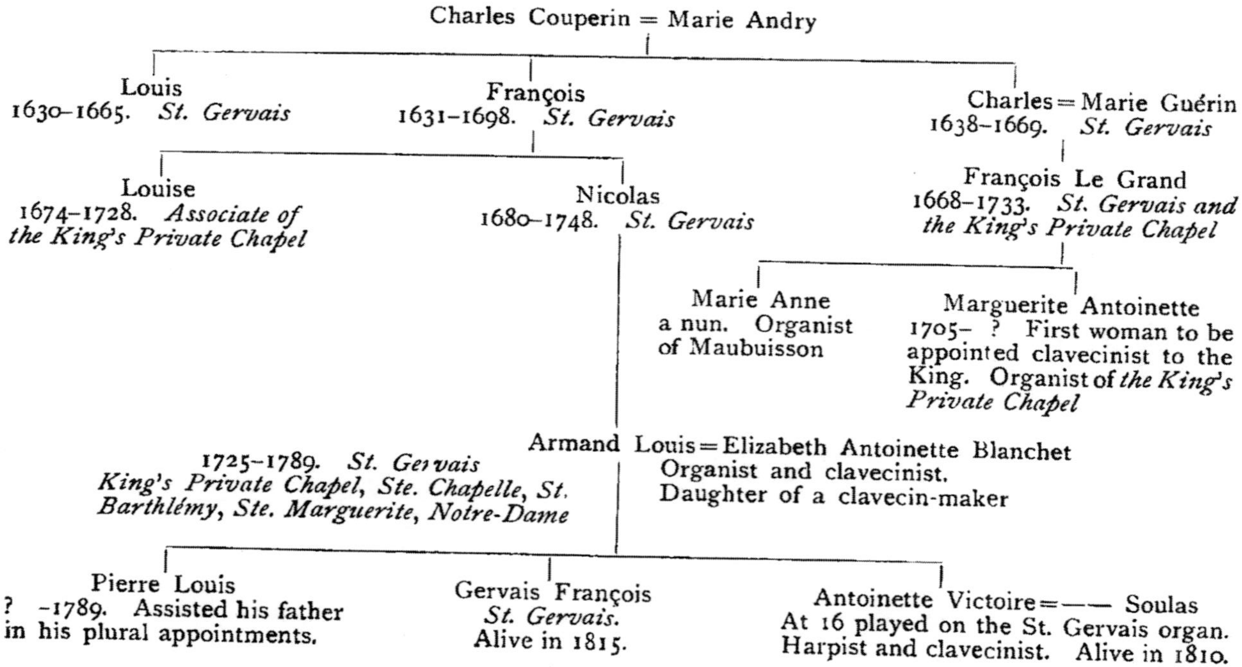

Note to the Couperin Pedigree.

The Couperin Pedigree is given on the opposite page, with the appointments held by various members of the family printed in italics. Galton's oversight is singular, for, after the Bachs, the Couperins appear to come next, in number, at any rate, and their retaining two posts in the family for nearly two hundred years is a remarkable instance of continuity of vocation. The dates are taken from *Grove*, and do not agree in every case with those in *Fétis*, *Gerber*, and the later and larger Biographies of *Michaud* (Paris, 1852), and *Hoefer* (Paris, 1855).

We should like to know a little about the terms on which the Couperins held their various appointments,—how much was due to talent, and how much to favouritism. It is significant that in his *Chapelle-Musique des Rois de France* (Paris, 1832), Castil-Blaze mentions only one of the family in a survey which begins with Clovis and ends with the state of music in the year 1832. On p. 160 he speaks of Mademoiselle Couperin as an accompanist at the Court of Louis XV. in 1749. She must be Marguerite Antoinette, daughter of Couperin Le Grand, and may have been referred to specially on account of her having been the first woman to hold this office.

Castil-Blaze gives lists of composers, conductors, instrumentalists, soloists and chorus, but not a word about the other Couperins who held Court appointments. Was it a tradition to have a Couperin at Court; was there influence or intrigue at work; was there possibly incompetence? Burney is not always a safe guide, but we have his assurance (*The Present State of Music in France and Italy*, 2nd edition, p. 40, London: 1773) that Armand Louis—not the nephew, as he calls him, but the second cousin, of the great Couperin—was a brilliant organist. He also seems to have been an unblushing pluralist.

At first sight this pedigree suggests heredity, but without evidence bearing upon outward and inward circumstances, we are not warranted in concluding that it is anything more than a good case of continuity of vocation.

It is worthy of note that this family of musicians, whatever the individual accomplishment of its members may have been, went its way quietly through nearly two centuries, looking on at the reigns of six Kings, two Regencies, a Revolution, a Convention, a Directory, a Consulate, an Empire, and a Downfall,—systems or consequences of Government surely various and experimental enough to satisfy the most exacting.

CHAPTER VIII

A CLINICAL STUDY

In modern times there is a blameworthy tendency to seek for abnormalities in the mental and physical condition of men who are engaged in artistic vocations, and attempts have been made to ascribe the faculty for creative work to some "taint." The result has been a host of misconceptions and inaccuracies, spread abroad by men who only too plainly have shown themselves unqualified for their task. Far too much ignorant attention has been given to the composer's psycho-physiological or psychopathic states, and it seems right to expose many erroneous impressions which already have gained widespread currency, and may now be too deeply rooted to be wholly eradicated.

Could I have avoided it I would have passed over those pseudo-scientific compilations which profess to make a clinical study of men who have distinguished themselves in art. It may be argued that the question is no urgent one, and that it is easy to discount irresponsible conclusions arrived at by men who have no qualifications for such investigations; but the matter cannot be dismissed so lightly. It has become the fashion to attach a stigma to those who have shown creative ability, and much anxiety has been displayed to discover in a man's private life the faintest sign which, in the opinion of a quite unskilled observer, may indicate a cerebro-spinal lesion. The dissemination of half-digested knowledge may do harm and lead to needless apprehension or great unhappiness, but whatever conclusions are drawn they should be left to that profession which alone is qualified to discuss and estimate them at their true value.

Where the layman, no matter how conscientious, fails is in his ignorance of the way in which morbid processes are connected with one another. Diminished acuity of vision arises in certain cases from a cause quite remote from the ocular apparatus: it may be the first sign of serious mischief elsewhere. A man may die of heart-failure when the seat of disease is in the lungs. "Inflammation of the brain" may be the result of pathological conditions in another region. "Apoplexy" does not invariably imply disease of the brain. The physician's first act, in the case of a "stroke," is to examine the heart and arteries. "Apoplexy" is not due to a defect in the brain, but to a change in the blood-vessels throughout the body.

The rupture of a blood-vessel may occur anywhere, but as the brain-substance has not the consistency that other organs have to support the impaired and friable walls of the arteries, these give way where there is the least resistance. As the brain controls the entire organism, no fatal result can attend mankind without involving in some way or other the cerebro-spinal system.

These facts are not to be realized by the casual attendance at some popular lectures on physiology, or by reading scientific text-books which cannot be understood except by those who have prepared themselves by a long study of the human frame under normal conditions.[1]

In the circulation of loose statements and wild assumptions there is much risk, not only to the public, but also to the artist. It is easy to leap to conclusions based upon bald generalizations which may be entirely imaginary or arrived at by friends who would like to be looked upon as confidants of those who had attained greatness. But some misunderstood

[1] Some years ago a teacher of "Voice-Production" published a book in which he professed to have invented an instrument based upon Marey's sphygmograph. By means of this he took what he imagined were graphic tracings of the vibrations of the vocal cords, and these he believed were indications of the manner in which the cords acted when notes and vowels were formed. He fixed his apparatus over the larynx, and obtained quite good and indubitable tracings of the carotid artery.

trait in an artist's life may convey a false impression, and may be the means of leading to the downfall of a youth who has modelled himself upon his hero. *Quod licet Jovi non licet bovi* is an aphorism which he may not have learnt, and the effect of untrustworthy gossip upon his character may be disastrous. Above all, there can be nothing more reprehensible than the practice of seeking in the life of an artist for some indication of an easy code of living or a moral flaw, for when one is found or imagined, it affords the young artist an example, and, what is worse, an excuse.

The question is a judicial one, and he who constitutes himself a Commission *de lunatico inquirendo* should act as if the liberty of every individual whom he discusses were at stake. The case, in fact, should be reported as minutely as if it were to be placed before a tribunal with immense issues to be decided.

In recent years a book called *The Insanity of Genius*[1] has had some vogue: it has reached a fifth edition, and has been referred to as a standard work. It is always an invidious task to deal with a dead author's opinions, but when they mislead through inadequate knowledge of the subject and are quoted as authoritative, some serious attention must be paid to them.

[1] J. F. Nisbet, *The Insanity of Genius and the General Inequality of Human Faculty Physiologically* (sic) *Considered.* Fifth edition (Lond. Moring, undated).

It may be urged that it is rather too late in the day to discuss a book whose preface was dated September, 1891, but as its conclusions are based upon the most meagre evidence, and as it has done an incalculable amount of harm, it cannot even now be passed over in silence. One does not question Nisbet's sincerity when he set out to prove his theory. How far he was equipped for his inquiry will be gathered from what follows here. No doubt his researches were adequately reviewed when they first appeared, and no general criticism will be resorted to now, but as the title of the book has become a catchword, and as its sub-title makes claims to absurd pretensions, some comment is necessary in connection with the purpose of the present work.

Nisbet is not the only writer who has singled out intellectual men for analysis: Lombroso and Nordau occur as examples;[1] but as Nisbet covers a special field and deals for the most part with names that are household words, it is fitting that we should give our attention to him.

It is unnecessary to discuss every "case" that he quotes: a few will be taken at random to show what reliance may be placed on his assertion that "the

[1] Lombroso is referred to later on p. 185. His conclusions have been challenged by many. In his pamphlet, *The Sanity of Art* (London, 1908), George Bernard Shaw has exposed the fallacies of Nordau.

general inequality of human faculty [has been] physiologically considered" by him, and then we will study the examples which the author professed to have discovered in the clinical records of composers.

Some notice must be taken of the practice of calling the alienist a "mad doctor." The use of this term, by men who set out to investigate the presence of mental disease, shows clearly in what category they are to be placed.

The Herschel family is discussed on pages 225 to 227. One would like to know, in passing, what inferences as regards "insanity" are to be drawn from the fact that one member died aged 82, and another aged 92, and that William Herschel married a woman who suffered from gout. What is interesting is the accurate description by Herschel the younger, a man trained to observe, of his attacks of hemicrania (or migraine) accompanied with the usual scotomata. The "fortifications" which presented themselves to him are typical of the visual phenomena which are present during the attack. Herschel's account is perfectly accurate, but the ocular disturbance was referable to a cause which does not concern the eye at all. Nisbet, however, speaks of the attacks as "curious sensorial hallucinations" which "accompanied the younger Herschel's genius," and apparently regards them as indicating some purely cerebral disturbance. A prosaic blue pill would have robbed these "hallucinations" of all their romance.

Again, on page 110, with regard to Milton's blindness, Nisbet states that "the seat of the evil was probably the optic nerves." That "probably" sheds an awkward light on his methods. But Milton himself, in *Paradise Lost*, Book III, line 25, describes his affection as a "drop serene," the literal translation of *gutta serena*, the old name for *glaucoma*,[1] a disease which does not primarily involve the optic nerve, and Nisbet's further statement that Milton's eyes "never showed any structural blemish" is exactly the description which we should have expected of some unskilled contemporary of the poet. To attribute Milton's being "physically undergrown" to the presence of a "neurotic condition" is sheer nonsense.

The chapter on Musicians begins with the unfortunate sentence: "Pathologically speaking, Music is as fatal a gift to its possessor as the faculty for poetry or letters; the biographies of all the greatest musicians being a miserable chronicle of the ravages of nerve-

[1] The word *glaucoma* occurs, and the disease is described, in a treatise, περὶ ὄψιος, at one time assigned to Hippocrates, but now admitted to be spurious. Be that as it may, as none of the doubtful Hippocratic Treatises are ascribed to writers of a period much later than the founding of the Alexandrine Library (*circ.* B.C. 320), the name and the recognition of the disease are of sufficient antiquity for our purpose.

disorder, extending, like the Mosaic curse, to the third and fourth generation." If Nisbet's conclusions were valid it would be possible to make out a case of insanity from "housemaid's knee."

This is Johann Sebastian Bach's "miserable chronicle." "The fatal inheritance of nerve-disorder first betrayed itself by shortsightedness in his youth." This should be cheering news for those affected with myopia, which has nothing whatever to do with "nerve-disorder," except in so far as all abnormal conditions must implicate the nervous system. Nisbet points out that the history of the ancestors of Bach is obscure, and goes on to say (page 164): "Yet the meagreness of the record does not disguise the growing ravages of nerve-disorder in their midst, the evil culminating . . . in the person of Sebastian Bach." From this one would look for a history of hopeless insanity. What are these "ravages of nerve-disorder"? "At sixty-five he became totally blind; a year later he was stricken with apoplexy, from which he died. Strange to say, ten days before his death, his sight was suddenly restored, from which it may be concluded that his blindness arose, not from a defect of the retina or a decay of the optic nerves, but from some disturbance of the visual centre (*sic*) of the brain, which the apoplexy temporarily corrected." Thus far Nisbet. As for the facts, Bach suffered from cataract, and was operated upon by

Taylor, an Englishman who travelled through Germany in 1750 and 1751. The method employed was known as "couching," by which the posterior capsule of the opaque lens was ruptured so as to allow the lens to fall back into the vitreous. By the removal of the opacity in this way light was admitted to the retina, but the patient could not perceive objects unless the absence of the lens from its normal position was compensated for by an artificial lens in front of the eye—by spectacles, in fact, of a certain power.

The opaque lens, in escaping into the posterior chamber or vitreous, lay in the only place for it, namely against the iris in the "danger-zone" of the eyeball, and acted as a foreign body. It is not to be wondered at that blindness resulted. Happily this crude procedure has long been abandoned, to the physical benefit of the patient and the moral advantage of the surgeon.

The blindness that followed was due either to traumatic glaucoma or to detachment of the retina. If the former, we should have had another kind of history, for the effects of traumatic glaucoma are too distressing to be overlooked even by the least skilled observer. The statements point to detachment, and this is confirmed by the reference to his "sight" having been "suddenly restored." This came about, not through apoplexy, but through the foreign body having been displaced so as to allow the fold of the retina, which had become detached from the sclerotic, to sink back into its normal position, and so let light reach the fundus.

What is certain is that his sight was not restored, but he may have had perception of light, which is not the same thing. It is also certain that the visual centres could not have been affected, for we should have had another chain of symptoms, equally well marked.

I have gone in detail into this "case" so that the reader may judge how far Nisbet is to be trusted when he talks of "ravages of nerve-disorder," and attempts to class Johann Sebastian with the other inmates of his curious asylum. There is not a shred of evidence to show that Bach had at any time the faintest symptoms of mental disease, while to say that these (non-existent) "ravages culminated" in him is as wicked as it is ignorant. If ever there was a composer sturdily sane in his surroundings and serenely at peace in the λατρεία of his work (in the Platonic sense), it was Johann Sebastian Bach.

This detachment of the retina, I may add, was the affliction of a well-known artist and man of letters, who had his moments of darkness and then his sight again, and I mention this fact here lest some one in days to come should attempt to draw perverted conclusions from the ocular affliction from which that upright and wholly sane gentleman, the author of *Trilby*, suffered.

Nisbet's next statement is that one of Bach's twenty children was an idiot boy. No one, with the most elementary knowledge of physiology (in the scientific, not the Nisbet sense), of the rearing of children, and of the processes that are suppressed during gestation, will be surprised to hear that most of the children died in childhood, or that they were overcome by the fate which is the usual lot of large families. But the statement establishes nothing as regards insanity or genius.

We come to Handel. His mother was "subject to paralytic seizures, in one of which she lost her sight" (page 165). "About the age of fifty Handel was himself struck down with paralysis, which so seriously unhinged his mind that for over a year he had to live in retirement."

Let us examine some dates. In the year 1737, at the age of 52, after a strenuous life, during which he produced some of his greatest work, Handel became bankrupt, owing to causes which did not involve his moral conduct in any way. His health naturally broke down, and he had an attack of paralysis, which forced him to go abroad. If it was a "stroke" it could not have been a severe one, for he was able soon after to undertake the serious business of a voyage to the Continent. He returned in the same year scarcely recovered, after barely six months in retirement, and had two new works ready for performance in the following spring, when a public monument was erected in his honour.

In this year, 1738, he composed two of his greatest works, *Saul* and *Israel in Egypt*. In the following year he composed the *Ode on St. Cecilia's Day*, and *L'Allegro*, and *Il Penseroso*. In 1742 he composed *The Messiah*. Again, in 1744-5, he was bankrupt, because he would not sin against his artistic conscience. In spite of these misfortunes he produced eight new works in the five following years.

He became blind from cataract, was couched by the same surgeon who had operated upon Bach, with the same result. But this crowning affliction was not enough to break the man, for he actually took part in the performances of his own works, and continued to do so till within eight days of his death, at the age of 74.

That is not the record of a man who suffered from the "ravages of nerve-disorder": it is the magnificent life-history of a man of the highest integrity, of indomitable purpose: it is the career of a man who must have possessed amazing energy and fortitude to begin his life over again, not once but twice, and at an age when most would have been too crushed by the blow ever to rise again. To be bankrupt at 60, to set to work again and to produce music which still lives, shows that Handel must have been endowed with a splendid mental and physical constitution.

The adversity against which Mozart had to fight —and his experiences were no exception—made it remarkable not only that he was able to work, but even to exist. We are told by Nisbet (page 167), that he died of "inflammation of the brain," but in *Grove*, second edition, iii. p. 300, "malignant typhus fever" is given as the cause of death, upon which the meningitis would supervene. The puffing out of the cheeks referred to in both books had nothing to do with the imitation of wind instruments: it is a well-known feature in certain states of coma.

In a consideration of Mozart's case, there is nothing which points to "ravages of nerve-disorder." He had a specially hard life, in which privations and poor hygienic surroundings exercised their fatal powers. Strangely enough there is nothing in the character of his music that reflects the hardships with which he had to contend, and if we knew him only through his music we should be disposed to say that it had been written by a man in placid and easy circumstances.

It must be admitted that in the case of Beethoven, the alienist might find grounds to support the view that the composer's mind was not far off the borderland. On page 167 it is stated that Beethoven died of dropsy. "More probably the vital functions were impaired through a deterioration of the brain." But we have a clinical history which is of value.[1] On December 2, 1826, he "caught a violent cold in the stomach," which "developed into an inflammation of the lungs, and on this dropsy supervened." He died on March 26, 1827, aged 57.

The report of the *post-mortem* examination will be taken in connection with the references to his deafness. Beethoven was 28 years of age when he first became aware of a defect in hearing. The cause was syphilis. Let us consider the special results. The composer, almost at the beginning of his career, finds that the sense that is most precious to him is impaired beyond all hope of recovery. As the years pass the disease declares itself in the liver, all the digestive functions are thrown out of order, his entire system is subject to its ravages. (The word is appropriate here.) The composer, therefore, has to fight against physical pain which seldom leaves him, and has to undergo constant mental suffering caused by his realizing that he is shut off from the sounds of the outer world, and even from those very sounds which he is creating in silence.

[1] *Grove*, 2nd edition, vol. i. p. 257. All the material here quoted appeared in the first edition of *Grove*, published in 1890, so there was no excuse in 1891 for Nisbet not consulting this authority.

Put any man into a like state of mind and body and attempt to picture what his life would be from day to day. It is little wonder that Beethoven was eccentric and irritable, that he was "always absent-minded and unpractical." We need not catalogue his "failings," but it is essential to point out that his "peculiarities" were not due to a primary cerebro-spinal lesion, but to an acquired taint which invaded one organ after another. The surprising thing is that in spite of his physical condition he was able to produce any work at all, and that he retained any of his faculties with a lesion of the ear which might have been accompanied with most distressing results. He must have possessed an extraordinary power of resistance, and an examination of the terrible consequences of what was then an ineradicable disease shows us that while bodily suffering was his in a measure that would have broken down many a man before the age of 57, he must have been endowed with an heroic endurance, a sublime consciousness, a true sanity, that helped him through his difficulties.

The chill that he caught caused acute renal disease, hence the dropsy, and with the poison already in his system the vitality of every organ was impaired. The inflammation of the lungs could not have been serious, for he lived nearly four months after the attack. From first to last, Beethoven's clinical history illustrates the usual course that his malady takes. The taint was an accident in his life, but it was not this that caused him to write music.

From the *post-mortem* appearances, Beethoven ought to have died insane. He did not, for he was quite clear in his mind till within two days of his death.

If Nisbet's statements are to be accepted without inquiry, the history of the Mendelssohn family is an extraordinary one. Every member seems to have been affected with some cerebro-spinal lesion, and if in Felix Mendelssohn-Bartholdy there was a "converging heredity of nerve-disorder" (p. 169), he certainly interrupted the bad family tradition. For whatever conclusions might have been drawn regarding the nerve-centres of his immediate relatives, there was nothing in his own to indicate degeneracy.

He was the first composer of any note whose worldly means sheltered him from the anxieties and privations so common in the lives of others following the same vocation. His well-being secured him against the struggle that has been the lot of most composers; his parents were in a good social position, and he was brought up in an atmosphere in which a strict code of life was observed. Into his short existence he crowded an enormous amount of work, and the work was good, considering its limitations. He was a voluminous letter-writer, a good draughtsman, and an accomplished painter. He was interested in mankind and the labours of others; his success and popularity were instantaneous and permanent, and he was a very machine of fastidiousness and method. We are assured that he was modest, that he was scrupulous in his dealings with men. He cultivated the affections in his own immediate circle, and was in all respects a pattern of everything that a good citizen should be. It is difficult to understand why Nisbet should have been at pains to catalogue the various infirmities of Mendelssohn's relatives, seeing that Mendelssohn himself showed no trace of taint.

His industry was colossal, his journeyings to and fro were incessant, and one asks how he had time to write a note of music. But he took too much upon himself and did not spare his energies. His visits to England were planned so that every hour was accounted for; he lived in a whirl of excitement, and when his brief life flickered out, it was because he killed himself with overwork. Always anxious to be at everybody's disposal, to ingratiate all and displease none, he thought too little of himself, and when the strain came he was not ready.

A few disappointments, a little penury, might have inured him to physical ills; he might have written less music and put more virility into it. But he died at 37 of the rarest of all maladies—success.

To take the other composers mentioned by Nisbet, Donizetti and Schumann died insane.[1] The facts are not in dispute, but it is right to point out that Schumann's insanity was due, not to disease of the brain, but to a point of pressure upon it. Had he lived in our own time, this point would have been immediately localized and removed, and he would have had a good chance of recovery. Weber, Hérold and Chopin died of tuberculosis, but Schubert (p. 172) was not "worn out at 31." He died of typhus, while Bellini died of what *Grove* calls "dysentery." In this small group the average age was only 40: we shall see presently how we stand as regards length of life.

Gluck, "avaricious and addicted to drink, died of apoplexy." But he died at the age of 73, and produced his last work at 65, not a bad record. Nisbet tells us that Rossini "at times laboured under the hallucination that he was miserably poor," an early warning of general paralysis. Lombroso is quoted as his authority. But for all that he managed to reach the age of 76. Balfe died of asthma at 62, his last

[1] "Je n'irai pas soutenir que Schumann doive son génie à son maladie: j'ai l'horreur de ces theories si laides qui servent aussi bien à décrier les hommes de génie qu'à exalter les criminels. Loin d'être une monstruosité morbide, le génie représente la santé suprême de l'esprit, un équilibre exceptionnel entre deux facultés, elles-mêmes exceptionnelles, d'impression et d'expression." Jean Chantavoine, *Musiciens et Poètes*. Paris: Alcan, 1912, p. 208.

work having been produced in the previous year. Berlioz died at 66, heart-broken over the failure of his last, and what he regarded as his greatest work, *Les Troyens*, which had been produced six years earlier.

Our last "case" given by Nisbet is Wagner. We are living too close to him, perhaps, to see his life in just proportion, but even with the enormous amount of material at hand regarding the most minute details of every moment of his existence, there is not a single circumstance that cannot be accounted for on perfectly rational grounds. What we have specially to note is that he was 56 years of age when his son was born, that he began his crowning work at 66, produced it at 69, and died of cardiac disease at 70. Granted that he was impatient and irascible, and frequently lost his self-control, we have to consider what gave rise to his well-known explosions of temper. Misunderstood and misrepresented, living in an environment in which he had to fight at every moment in defence of the faith that was in him, he was not unnaturally jealous for his work, and violent when provoked by the stupidity of criticism.

It would be strange indeed were we to assign to an impairment of the nervous system the fury and indignation that many a man displays without one-tenth of the provocation and still less of the justification that wrought Wagner to heights of anger. Not many men would have acted to their wives as he did to Minna, with her dulness of wit and uninspiring presence, for in spite of all differences he showed himself ever anxious for her comfort. The nervous tension of having to work—and his task was superhuman—in an atmosphere of bickerings, with a jealous woman as a thorn in his side, together with his straitened means, would have driven many another, less self-reliant and strong, to a pitiful end.

The petty incidents of many a life may be exaggerated into undue importance, but here we are dealing with a question of grey matter, as I said at the outset, and whatever Wagner may have been in his intimate relations with those who at any time were part of his household, the chief point to consider is what effect these relations had upon his daily work. We are therefore forced to the conclusion that the strain of Music was so potent within him that no outward circumstances or trivialities influenced his productive faculties. The inference is that, unstable as he might appear to have been in domestic matters and concerns, his mind was so stable as regards his art that it went its way, steadily and consistently, unaffected by the outbursts which apparently were inevitable when he was brought back to earth in an encounter with the *petit ménage.*[1]

[1] The above was written before the publication of Ernest Newman's *Wagner as Man and Artist* (London, 1914). His analysis,

These, then, are the cases upon the strength of which Nisbet based his assertions that "the biographies of all the greatest musicians are a miserable chronicle of the ravages of nerve-disorder." He names seventeen, only two of whom can be classed as insane, and of the hundreds of composers known to the world, there are only three authenticated cases that I have encountered. No doubt among less conspicuous men cases of insanity have occurred, but in these the "blot upon the brain" may have been caused by irregularities of living, and would show itself no matter what their vocation was. In the case of the composer, Nisbet endeavoured to show some relation of genius to insanity. He had an immense field in which to search for examples, but he failed in his "miserable chronicle."

I have pointed out the special pleading which resulted in his drawing far-fetched conclusions, while at the same time I have given the opinion which a medical man would pass on the facts laid before him.

strictly judicial in temper and patient in research, puts Wagner's psychology at last in its true light, and although Mr. Newman has traced the master's character from a point of view different from mine at this place, I see no reason for reconsidering my remarks. One quotation from this admirable study must suffice. "His art absorbed the whole of his nature. He knew what he wanted to do, and what he needed in order to do it, and for him to need a thing and to insist on having it were mental processes hardly separable from one another" (p. 43).

If the old records had been kept with care, and if diagnostic methods had been as rigorous and minute as they are now, the past might have rendered an account more grievous than that which we have just analysed. As to this we cannot speak, for we do not know. But to end the discussion of this book, it is clear that no advocate ever went into court with so sweeping an indictment, and with so little to substantiate it.

It would be practically impossible single-handed to investigate every incident in the lives even of the most conspicuous composers, but in connection with this inquiry we may consider the ages of some. The names are those given in the chart at the end of *The Threshold of Music*, starting from the year 1500. The chart was designed to illustrate a point with which we have nothing to do at present, but as it comprises composers identified with the progress of Music at every stage, it supplies us with a typical group. As the list was compiled in connection with a different branch of research, I am absolved from any charge of having selected my cases.

The first table gives the names and ages of composers who died under 50, and their fatal diseases, as far as it has been possible to ascertain them. The average age is 39.9.

TABLE III. Names and ages of composers who died under 50.[1]

Cesti	49 ?	
Peri	49 ?	
Locke	47 ?	
Morley	46	In ill health for last five or six years of life.
Arcadelt	46 ?	
Schumann	44	Mental disease.
O. Gibbons	42	Apoplexy.
Weber	40	Tuberculosis.
Chopin	40	Tuberculosis.
Mendelssohn	37	Ascribed to "apoplexy." (Cardiac disease ?)
Bizet	37	Cardiac disease.
Purcell	37	Tuberculosis ?
Mozart	35	Typhus.
Bellini	34	"Dysentery." (Enteric ?)
Schubert	31	Typhus.
Pergolesi	26	"Apparently notoriously profligate" and tubercular (*Grove*, 2nd ed. vol. iii. *s.v.*).

What strikes us at first sight in the above list is the large number of deaths ascribed to diseases

[1] Nisbet refers to Hérold, who died at the age of 42 of tuberculosis. He does not mention Goetz (1840-1876), who died of the same disease, aged 36. These are not included here, because I am taking only the names in the Chart as the basis of a broad test. On this principle I have excluded Auber (89), Spontini (77) and Spohr (75), whose average age of 80 would have influenced the results of Table IV.

Smetana (1824-1884) also died insane. A peculiar feature of his deafness has been referred to on p. 92.

now classed as infective, and therefore preventable. Tubercle claims its toll, a high one, if the records are to be trusted, but this is not to be wondered at when it occurs in men following a sedentary calling. In an age when sanitary measures are better understood, and consequently enforced, the likelihood is that typhus and enteric would not have been met with, while tubercle would have been "taken in time."

In this list, always on the assumption that we can rely upon the statements at hand, it is worthy of note that of those composers whose fatal diseases are given, the majority would have had a fair chance of recovery had they been born in our generation.

In Table IV. there are 54 composers who died over the age of 50. The average age of these is 67.3, no less than 17 years above the age of the youngest in the list, thus showing that there is a preponderance of ages above the average, sufficient to bring those far below the average up to the mean.

If we take Tables III. and IV. together, we find that of a number of composers chosen from a list which has nothing to do with duration of life and has a range of four hundred years, only 23 per cent. died under the age of 50. The average age of all the composers instanced is 61, or 21 years above the average age of those in Table III.

TABLE IV. Names and ages of composers who died over 50.

Verdi	88	O. di Lasso	67
Schütz	87	H. Lawes	67
Cherubini	82	V. Galilei	67
Rameau	81	Berlioz	66
Byrd	80	Scarlatti, (A.)	66
Galuppi	79	John Bull	66
Tartini	78	Bach	65
Haydn	77	Couperin	65
Cavalli	76 ?	Brahms	64
Rossini	76	Grieg	64
Monteverde	76	Dowland	63
Liszt	75	Dvořák	63
Gounod	75	Boccherini	62
Handel	74	Offenbach	61
Gluck	73	Corelli	60
Meyerbeer	73	Smetana	60
Piccinni	72	Sweelinck	59
Grétry	72	Sullivan	58
Tallys	70	Beethoven	57
Wagner	70	W. Lawes	55 ?
Carissimi	70	Field	55
Lalo	69	Lully	54
Philidor	69	Glinka	54
Boyce	69	Tschaikovsky	53
Palestrina	68	Borodin	53
Franck	68	Donizetti	51
Arne	68	Cavalieri	50 ?

These figures are instructive, for the men to whom they refer belong for the most part to a period when knowledge of medicine and sanitation were against rather than in favour of long life. The inference is that in spite of the conditions popularly associated with it, the life of a composer is quite "good" from the point of view of assurance, and will compare favourably with the lives of those following less hazardous vocations.

This must be sufficient for the present purpose, but it must not be forgotten that age alone is not an infallible test. In our own time we are conniving at the survival of the unfittest in our hospitals, work-houses and asylums, and in the last two kinds of institution there are always to be found instances of extreme old age.

Many of the composers mentioned died in harness, working up to the last in a high state of efficiency, and this fact in itself should rebut those thoughtless and pernicious assertions that in the vocation of Music there is a persistent and ineradicable strain of mental and physical deterioration.

I have not thought it necessary to refer to Lombroso's work, *The Man of Genius*,[1] for the reason that a large collection of isolated statements about men known to the world is a frail foundation upon which to build

[1] Lombroso, *The Man of Genius*, London, 1891.

any theory whatsoever. According to him, no one has escaped some taint; but as he mentions hundreds of men who have gained their immortality and not a few whose claims to that distinction are somewhat slender, it is manifestly impossible that he could have tested each case for himself. In many instances he accepts evidence which is little else than gossip.[1]

It is undoubted that the alienist and neurologist can diagnose much from one single authenticated symptom without seeing the patient, just as the biologist can make valuable deductions from the study of a single bone. But this is far removed from the "proof" of degeneration adduced by Lombroso in the case of Mozart (p. 34), who, "in carving meat, so often cut his fingers, accustomed only to the piano, that he had to give up this duty to others."

In his exhaustive analysis of the main traits of the men and women whose lives are recorded in the *Dictionary of National Biography*, Havelock Ellis remarks,[2] "The association of genius with insanity is not, I believe, without significance, but in face of the fact that its occurrence is only demonstrable in less than

[1] In *The Man of Genius* (1st English edition, Schwerin, I.M., 1914) Türck says: "A complete refutation of Lombroso's hypothesis would mean the production of a vast library" (p. 323); and refers to "the large amount of quite uncritically sifted material adduced in his works as evidence" (p. 317).

[2] Havelock Ellis, *A Study of British Genius*, London, 1904, p. 191.

5 per cent. cases, we must put out of court any theory as to genius being a form of insanity." He quotes the "bold" assertion of Dr Maudsley[1] "that there is hardly ever a man of genius who has not insanity or nervous disorder of some form in his family,"—an assertion which holds good of many who are not geniuses,—and significantly comments on the fact that "it is nearly twenty years since that statement was made, yet neither Dr. Maudsley nor anyone else has yet brought forward any sound evidence in support of it."

It is not difficult to comprehend the reluctance of alienists to discuss or to refute in print wild exaggerations, for were they to do so they would be compelled to adduce cases within their own experience, the description of which might afford clues to the identity of their patients. Mental peculiarities can be observed by friends whose evidence is recognized by the law of England, and these characteristics would be more easily detected than the record, in a medical journal, of an unusual operation, the details of which would be known only to the surgeon and his assistants. The alienist's mouth, therefore, is shut, and his reticence is not blameworthy.

I will leave this subject with a further reference to Havelock Ellis, whose judicial attitude in this matter

[1] H. Maudsley, *Heredity in Health and Disease*, *Fortnightly Review*, May, 1886.

is in strong contrast with that of the late Professor of Criminal Anthropology at the University of Turin. He says, on p. 194, "Even if there is a slightly unusual liability to insanity among men of genius, there is no general tendency for genius and insanity, even when occurring in the same individual, to be concomitant. . . . Periods of insanity may alternate with periods of high intellectual achievement, but the two states are not concomitant, and genius cannot be accurately defined as a disease."

We may all end our days in asylums, but that will not prove that we were geniuses.

CHAPTER IX

MAN AND HIS ART

It may be admitted that there are many traits in an artist's character which we should like to overlook, but in this respect we have the same to say of not a few of those with whom we are in contact, socially and commercially. Character, fortunately, can never be standardized: accordingly there is always scope for the individual whose weaknesses and failings after all add to the colour, the interest, the pageantry of life more than his impervious probity or his unctuous rectitude.

It is a toss-up between scamp and saint, and however we may deplore the proceedings of the one and commend the fervour of the other, the issue in the end lies with those who have compassed all the gamut of human experience and emotion. Many a scamp has won canonization by a panic-stricken "conversion" on his death-bed; many a saint has given his whole life to the faith that was in him, without a conspicuous or even derogatory occurrence to call attention to the matter that he had in hand, and has gone to his grave in quietness, as all saints go.

The question that we have to examine is whether there are traits in the artist which are specially developed in connection with his work. This is a matter as much for the physician as the psychologist, but it may be outlined here.

The artist in his relation to his surroundings is imperfectly understood. In order to produce his work under the most favourable and advantageous circumstances he requires conditions and an environment which to the plain man appear absurd or extravagant. The plain man, while ready to enjoy the work that the artist produces, is apt to brush aside all that led up to its creation.

The artist, too, is rarely unconscious that he is possessed of a mental endowment which puts him on a different plane from his fellows, and if he has enthusiasm and a strain of originality, his bearing and conversation are apt to be misjudged. From the earliest, unless he has an unusual amount of self-control, his efforts are directed towards his work being recognized, and as it is fairly certain that fame will not burst upon him in a morning, he finds himself taking arms against the common foe, Stupidity. No matter what renown he may eventually win, from start to finish his work and his life will be engaged in a perpetual struggle against the Enemy.

It is the fate of all creative and constructive minds. Jenner, Lister, and Mendel had to endure as much as Rodin, Whistler, and Wagner. The difference in temperament between the two groups was due to the nature of the material which they handled and also to the severe technical training that disciplined the men of science, a training which in the case of the artists was replaced by long periods of abstraction, of study of the accomplished work of others, and of patient and solitary practice. There was this further difference that the results of science were at least comprehensible and their sociological and commercial value could be demonstrated, while the artists themselves were regarded as incomprehensible and their labours of no utility.

It must be made clear that no defence is entered here for that state of mind classed under the much-abused phrase, "artistic temperament," which too often has been used to account for, or, more correctly, to explain away, impulsiveness, irresponsibility, and lack of self-control. In its popular application it refers to a phase of mental weakness rather than of strength, under the old idea that the artist was to be indulged by a freedom from social and moral codes which would be enforced in any other vocation.

Those who possess it in its finer meaning are content to show it in their work, and do not make it an excuse for their being a law, not only unto themselves, but largely also unto their relatives and friends.

In his campaign against Stupidity the artist, more especially at the outset of his career, resorts to "shock-tactics"—in a double sense—as much to stagger the adversary by force of impact as to offend his susceptibilities. The tactics, however, may degenerate into bad manners or a parade of disordered habits, but we cannot justly blame him if an inoffensive aloofness and isolation are the consequences of his being driven in upon himself.

The commercial man, who takes infinite care that his own environment shall be arranged and adjusted for the performance of his day's work in the way most advantageous to himself, is unable to understand that the artist has also *his* day to consider, and that he has no clerks, stenographers, typewriters, or telephones to help him. The prevalent idea is that he amuses himself by producing work which nobody wants, and that when he is good-humouredly taxed with his idleness he is impelled to do something *pour épater les bourgeois*.

The lack of sympathy and of generous understanding, persistent detraction and hostile criticism (the more cruel because it is so often anonymous), have many a time done more injury to a delicate and sensitive temperament than unsavoury surroundings and ill-chosen companions.

Another point to be remembered is that the artist is not a machine; he cannot enter the studio, as the banker does his chambers, and find the day's work either already in progress or carefully prescribed for him. The painter who is most fertile in invention and creation, who is never in want of a commission, not infrequently finds himself perilously near becoming a machine, and cases have been known of "popular" artists deliberately renouncing a class of their work much in demand for fear of losing that elasticity and swiftness of response to delicate stimuli which they knew were indispensable.

The sculptor and the painter, besides, have from a practical point many obstacles in their way. They have their materials to arrange and set out for the day's work, for the studio-assistant is a luxury enjoyed only by those who happily have reached fame. After developing a train of thought and concentrating his attention on the work that is to do, the artist may find his preparations upset by the failure of a model to keep an appointment, by the unpunctuality or lack of intelligence of a sitter, by the indifference of the light, by seeming trifles which upset the mind when it has been adjusted for a definite purpose. The working hours are limited by the seasons of the year and states of the weather. The carefully projected labours of a week may be deranged by some small incident. At all turns the human equation has to be reckoned with, as well as the enforced idleness when the light is gone, those hours that are dreaded by the artist who cares for nothing but his work and bitterly deplores the inaction and loss of time.

These may appear insignificant, but they are irksome to the artist, who has to think quite as much as other people, and deliberately brings his mind into tune with the task that is before him. Habit, no doubt, and the large satisfaction of handling his materials, may unconsciously create a mood which in those of a placid disposition scarcely varies from day to day, and the sight of a new canvas or of a lump of clay may provide the stimulus. The survey of work brought forward to a definite stage may suggest fresh developments, and the discipline to which he has been submitting insensibly while laying the foundations of his work takes command and in obedience he moves forward.

These small matters of detail have their uses, and there is never an effort without compensation. To a highly-strung man the routine of arranging his paints and brushes may be irritating, but it causes a temporary break which he does not notice so much because it is part of his work. The literary man, in his rush to spin out many thousand words per week

—a hideous method of reckoning—resorts to strange devices, and by acquiring the knack of dictating into a machine (and much actually reads as if it had been written for the edification of a piece of clockwork), loses the use of his hands. The essayist of a more leisurely period had his quill pens to make, the little interruption allowed him to think, and the distraction caused by the play of the small muscles of the hands rested the brain and gave time for the search for the fitting word.

In the case of the musician, mental and physical tension is brought to an extreme, and the combination of faculties for the study and performance of a large composition, such as a concerto, is extremely complex. Apart from the muscular exertion and the training involved, the sheer thought that has to be concentrated into three-quarters of an hour in the playing of it is bound to produce a reaction which many audiences forget when they thoughtlessly insist upon a preposterous number of recalls and an encore. The average day of a pianist amounts to eight hours, and whether he is in the first flight or among the rank and file he cannot take a rest. His work depends, from beginning to end, on irreproachable technique combined with all the mental qualities that may be classed as "interpretation" and "insight."

Taking this strain into account, we cannot wonder that he seeks diversion and distraction which in many instances assume a form as violent as the exertion demanded by his work. Thus it was that Liszt and Rubinstein, outside their public performances and public studies, led such strenuous lives, packed full of interest and excitement. Rest to them meant mental stimulus in another form. The physiology and psychology of the process in their cases are obvious.

The composer is placed in the most difficult position of all, for the organism upon which he depends is much at the mercy of his surroundings. He has to sustain an effort of concentration extending over long periods of time, and anything that intercepts or interrupts the flow of his ideas may be to him as serious as a financial crisis or an accident would be to some one else. The unexpected opening of a door or the sudden torture of a piano-organ may dissipate in an instant thoughts that he has been nursing and dwelling upon in silence for a long time. It may take days to recover from this instantaneous relaxation of the tension, or the balance may be restored in a moment.

Let us examine this matter of "mental balance," an expression which is often loosely employed without much attention to its meaning. In general it is taken to imply an orthodox way of thinking or a correct observance of conventions. More precisely it means that stability of character in which the elements of living are kept in due relation and proportion. It denotes the pursuit of an art, the greatest of all, the Art of Life, and may be summed up as the personal expression of fastidiousness and consistency.

Now it is illogical to condemn an artist for want of mental balance, if at the same time he is not allowed the environment, the atmosphere in which the equipoise is undisturbed.

Vocations of all kinds, especially those which have a purely worldly end in view, are invariably followed under conditions specially adapted to their successful pursuit, and those who engage in them are not usually submitted to a running fire of derogatory comment from their friends and the outside world. Their minds, further, are not violently predisposed towards their business; they are not actuated by irresistible impulses which drive them to defy parliamentary restrictions by keeping their shops open all night and all day.

The artist's chief business is to choose, from what he thinks and sees, everything that contributes to his work. Conventions of all kinds he rejects, because they are no concern of his; they do not *compose*, and as his attitude towards conventions in his work is strictly analytical and severely critical, he gradually assumes a like position towards those which he has to encounter in his life. This selective faculty is not bestowed upon all artists in equal strength. It is easy to note its presence or absence by the subject-matter of pictures on the walls of a gallery, or by the words that a composer sets to music. Technically the artist in any calling must be endowed with it, for by it alone is he able to judge how to develop his theme, what to leave out, when to stop, and it may be that he devotes so much attention to the equilibrium of his work that he has no time or inclination to consider conventional equilibrium in his way of life.

His own rules, under which he produces his work, may be so inflexible that in his private life he may demand compensation in the shape of a disregard for conventions, the strict observance of which by others less imaginative than himself, may seem to him infinitely smaller in importance and vastly easier to comply with, than the rigid canons which he has prescribed for himself.

Art in any form implies asceticism—not scented, plump æstheticism—but self-denial in one direction, exaltation in another. Ordeals of self-mortification at no time in the world's history stood for vivid activity or for life itself. They may have won some selfish advantage, some personal glorification, but they have a place alone, meaningless and purposeless.

Closely related to mental balance is habit. The man who is always producing something requiring concentration, cultivates an attitude of mind which becomes constant, and the variation is slight. The balance, as it were, swings within a small arc, and is not subjected to those violent oscillations which occur when work is carried on by fits and starts. The mind becomes accustomed to a discipline analogous to the regulated physical functions, and the more closely mind and body correspond with and respond to one another the greater and more lasting will be the stability.

It is not necessary here to consider the utility of an artist's work: we are more concerned with the urgency to himself that he should produce it. He may be oblivious of the demands of the outside world and of the ultimate destiny of his endeavours, but he is supremely conscious of the importance of occupying himself with the form of energy which he has found essential for his existence.

In every art we meet with what have been called "monuments of misapplied labour," but though the expression may be fitting in spite of its harshness, we ought to view the works to which it refers, not so much in relation to other and more successful efforts, as in relation to the quality of the mind that found something to do, even though it did it badly. We might then discover that we had to deal with a matter more profound than the making of bad works of art, we should be brought face to face with the creative instinct and all that it implies.

It has been pointed out[1] that man is endowed with the instinct for workmanship, and Loeb[2] in referring to this observes: "One of the most important instincts is usually not even recognized as such, namely the instinct of workmanship." He continues: "Lawyers, criminologists, and philosophers frequently imagine that only want makes man work. This is an erroneous view. We are instinctively forced to be active in the same way as ants or bees. The instinct of workmanship would be the greatest source of happiness if it were not for the fact that our present social and economic organization allows only a few to satisfy their instinct."

This is the driving force behind the artist. It accounts for much, though it does not wholly explain why men are willing to undergo privations and hardships in order that they may obey some inexplicable command from within.

It is conceivable that a man may follow an artistic career without having evinced any marked inclination for it in early years. Many, no longer in their "twenties," have been able, by dint of laborious practice, to overcome the disadvantages of having no

[1] Veblen: *The Theory of the Leisure Class*. New York, 1899.

[2] Loeb: *Comparative Physiology of the Brain and Psychology*. Lond. 1901, p. 197.

natural gift, but the results, except in literature, are almost invariably journeyman-work. There are examples, indeed, of men who, with a great love of Music, "took up the piano," as the phrase runs, in middle life, and by unlimited patience and perseverance were able to extend their knowledge and derive much pleasure. These cases, interesting as they are, do not concern us here, for the artistic impulse in them is not innate but mimetic.

On the other hand, we have men who deliberately repressed an artistic faculty till they felt the moment was ripe for it being given rein—the pre-eminent example is Michelangelo—but they were closely associated with other arts, and had studied deeply the way by which all arts impinged upon one another as an expression of personal observance or experience, and chose that particular form in which their thoughts had most scope and freedom.

For the artist is he who selects, who discerns that which is most fitting, and the failures are not to be ascribed to technical imperfections in the mode of expression in one medium, but rather to an inability to decide what medium is best fitted for the complete command of the thought.

This discernment is apt to be misunderstood or misjudged, if not condemned, by those who are incapable of appreciating it, and often ill-considered and harsh criticisms are passed upon those who, having minds of their own, exercise their powers of selection.

Art is experience, fitness, completion. The painter who feels that his thought can be better expressed in a sonnet is not to be remonstrated with because he does not limit himself to paint. No one interferes with him in his recreations: why castigate him for aiming at being an artist in all things and for having the gift, reprehensible in the eyes of some, of dual means of expression? The materialism of the present age is oddly inconsistent. The all-round man in sport or in business is belauded: but the all-round man of art is decreed by blind mouths to be spendthrift of brains if he writes music when they think he ought to be painting pictures, and if he chooses for self-expression the particular form of art which will represent that self-expression in the most complete form as he sees it. There is no "close time" for art, and those who would prescribe it overlook the fact that he is happiest and nearest grace who can pack into the shortness of his life as much of the length and breadth of art as he can—that is, his own experience, his sense of fitness and completeness.

Difficult as it may be for the humdrum person to understand why art is an absorbing passion, it is to be pointed out that every living thing is normal when in its own environment. The artist may be an enigma to the humdrum person: the humdrum person may be an enigma to the election-agent, and by passing from one to another we compass the social scale. Each, however, is normal provided that the accessories, the pabulum suitable for the environment, are at hand. But it is the composer who is an αἴνιγμα to himself, for he speaks in riddles, darkly, like the poet who takes a day, and more, to understand what he has written over-night.

Like a minute organism the composer sets apart something of himself: tends it: endows it with the life that is his own: nourishes it with all his strength: watches the budding of new faculties, new gifts: then when the hour is come he wounds himself to set it free, and lets it go forth to justify its existence.

It is significant that the artist is better understood by the medical man than by those in other professions and callings, chiefly for the reason that the profession of medicine has its two great branches, the Art of Physic, and Chirurgery, which is the work of the hands. Every physician or surgeon is more or less of a draughtsman, and if he is not, he must have that combination of observation and memory which he begins to cultivate at the outset of his training—two faculties indispensable to the sculptor and painter. In Music too the medical man does not fall short of those of his brethren who have excelled in other directions, and the manual dexterity gained in early years from the invaluable education to be obtained from practising musical instruments is never lost on those who must use their hands.

Besides this, there is that sympathy and comprehension of difficulties and failings which must arise in those who are daily in contact with human nature at its worst; often, too—for the glory of man—at its best.

It is because these two great missioners, the medicine-man and the artist, have a common aim in the scheme of humanity that they understand, better than any, the instinct for workmanship.[1]

There is yet another aspect of the composer. Regarding his gift in the light of a grave responsibility, a view of which unfortunately not too many are conscious, we find that the demands upon the intellect are so exacting, that if we did not feel—and this perhaps goes deeper than we may think—that Nature, by some wonderful adjustment, had provided against the contingency of perpetual tension in one direction, we might assert that no human faculty was capable of resisting the effort that the composer must put forth. His work calls for great powers of absorp-

[1] Duke Louis Ferdinand of Bavaria is Professor of Practical Surgery in the General Hospital of Munich, and also a first violin in the orchestra of the Prinz-Regenten Theater. It has been said of him that he never brought the life of a patient in jeopardy through a slip of his scalpel, and never tortured the ear of his Kapellmeister with the shadow of a discord.

tion and concentration, not exercised during short and interrupted periods, but sustained for days and weeks at a time for the production of one composition alone. He must see it complete, and never lose touch with the ordered plan, keeping before him proportion and contrast in the mental design which from its nature cannot be comprehended at a glance. He cannot leave one section and pass on to another; he has to compose as if his audience were listening. He is not like the artist who, on varnishing day, can change the whole complexion of his canvas, or as Turner did, repaint—without permission—neighbouring pictures which clashed with his own. His memory must be capable of retaining a multitude of details which cannot be noted in an instant, for the writing of a single bar in a full score is not like the writing of a word of three or four syllables in a sentence. In orchestral music he has to realize in an instant a dozen or more different timbres of sound, to analyze them and allocate each to its appropriate instrument, at the same time bearing in mind all the technical possibilities and limitations of those that he is employing.

In the maturing of a musical idea in silence the effort of abstraction is equally intense, and the slightest occurrence which interrupts the continuity of thought must react upon the brain.

From the special mental endowment which he

must possess before he can produce a phrase of music, he must experience moments of exaltation and emotion which isolate him from his surroundings. These are common to all who have recourse to their imagination, and vary in degree according to the intensity of the mental effort.

Particularly in Music, when he cannot immediately realize the effect of what he has written, the composer is less well off than the sculptor and painter who see their results as their work progresses. But the composer of an orchestral score may have to wait years before he has a chance of hearing and coming intimately in contact with his conception. Liszt heard his *Todtentanz* for the first time fifty-one years after it was written ; political troubles prevented Wagner from hearing *Lohengrin* till fifteen years after it was finished.

Thus there are elements in the composer's work which are not comparable with anything in another vocation, save possibly in architecture, when the creator of the design is impatient to see his work complete. But here the composer has the advantage in one respect at least : he can always destroy his score : the architect cannot rebuild.

The composer is conscious that in his own environment he and his brother-artists form a very small group in comparison with men engaged in other occupations, and that there is nothing in theirs that throws light upon his own. A man need not be a practising lawyer or a physician in order to understand simple points in jurisprudence or medicine, and to appreciate to some extent the attitude that these men take towards their work. The educated man is not completely at sea during a discussion about science, commerce, scholarship or literature, and he has at least a little comprehension of the fine arts. But in Music, especially in composition, there is much that is hidden, even from those engaged in it day by day, and it is this that constitutes the barrier.

The composer's mental equipment and surroundings should be studied as carefully as the outfit of an Arctic explorer must be, but whether we find fault with one peculiarity or another, in justice we must ask ourselves how we ourselves would act if in the prosecution of our ordinary tasks we had to encounter similar physical and mental obstacles.

At no time in the world's history has imagination played so great a part as it is doing now. The artist is not to be found only in the studio, the picture gallery, the concert room. He has invaded the dockyard, the machine-shop, the laboratory. The botanist and geologist, the chemist and electrician, are no longer looked upon as amiable but rather unbalanced faddists. They, too, like the artist, had to win their scars in the fight against prejudice and the vast host of the preoccupied, who declared that what was goodly in their fathers' eyes was goodly in theirs also, and that there was no room for change. But the creations of these men are tangible, and there is much virtue in their labours when the result is stated in the form of a balance-sheet, the hapless destiny of all great enterprises nowadays.

The composer is entitled to take his stand with them and to be judged with them. He should not be driven to a refuge within himself, with all the perils that come of introspection and solitude, or to bow down to false gods. The strain to which he submits is no greater than that which many a bridge-builder, many an engineer, many a surgeon, has to undergo in the course of his work, with the lives that depend upon him. It is no greater; it is only different.

But it is idle to insist that creative and imaginative work goes with an ill-balanced mind. Neither art nor science proceeds upon such an assumption.

Indeterminate as the position and value of art may still be in the conventional view of man's purpose, and difficult as many find it to give a reason for its necessity, it is clear that it is needful to the artist himself. That alone matters. The interviewer and the press-agent, the photographer and the picker of brains, have brought into the public gaze many who followed an artistic career, not from necessity but for self-advertisement. The time-server is preoccupied with what others think about himself, not with what he ought to be thinking about his work. To others in a more enviable frame of mind, work is joyous, alert, open-eyed, splendid. Masterpieces are no longer the flatulent inspirations of a broken heart: style can be cultivated and matured on something more substantial than the fare of the garret. Natural, not intensive, exuberance is true growth and sanity.

It has yet to be shown, and this will be the business of a later generation, whether art has gained or lost by the naked light of publicity which has been cast upon it. The question is too large, too serious to be gone into now; but the consoling fact for every creative artist to keep in mind is, that no matter what he or any of his contemporaries may accomplish in a brief hour, Time and Mankind alone are the grand Inquisitors. Great painters, great sculptors, have come and gone. Among artists their renown is imperishable, far out of reach of the vulgar estimate of the auction-room, or the ignorant cupidity of the millionaire.

But Music is above whims and fashions: no man can make it what it is not. The modest organist of the fifteenth century is still with us because he wrote something from his heart, and, so doing, touched other hearts, for Music that "goes home" stays there.

In the short history of Music there have been many glittering stars, men who were acclaimed in their own day and won the highest rewards. They gained too much in their life-time, for they are forgotten, like Le Sueur, the most honoured in France in the time of the Great Napoleon, now merely a name in a biographical dictionary, not even a finger-post in sound.

Many a composer has spent himself in reams: the names that are great now may not be great hereafter. An air of immortality may invest the endless procession of Madonnas in the Brera, but who remembers the name of their painters?

Time alone makes no concessions. Vast oscillations of nationalities and peoples have to be reckoned; tribal custom and race are being diluted and infiltrated to such an extent that tradition and pure breed are being elbowed out.

Man in the Occident is becoming mongrel.

The instinct for work keeps the world busy, and the primal instinct of which we have any evidence now is what we at present call Art. As the great mantle of ice receded from off the face of Europe, some hundreds of thousands of years ago, the cave-man, dependent upon his eyes and ears for his very existence, was alert and observant. Far in the narrowness of his dwelling he noted on its rocky walls what he had seen, and Time the All-knowing secured his drawings in the blackness of countless centuries against the hour when a race should come forth to stand amazed before the handiwork of a broad-nosed, prognathous savage (as he would be called), whose mastery of hand and eye were proved illimited ages ago.

Of late years much attention has been given to prehistoric man. The dimensions of his brain have been estimated and disputed; his very jaw[1] has caused as much commotion among scientific men as that *maxilla asini hemioni inferior* did in the hands of Samson with fabulous efficiency.

But apart from arguments and contentions, all that we know of *homo sapiens* is that he was an artist.[2]

Through the haze of controversy we can ascertain facts, and what we know of life in remote ages is based, not upon customs, traditions or religions, but upon drawings and sculpture, the accurate records of a phase of existence which, through their variety and artlessness, challenge that tangle known nowadays as civilization.

[1] Buttel-Reepen: *Man and his Forerunners*, Lond. 1913, p. 41.

[2] The question is fully discussed by Spearing in his *Childhood of Art*, Lond. 1913.

BIBLIOGRAPHY

This Bibliography does not profess to be anything more than an outline. References to Music in psychological works in the English language are few. One of the leading authorities naïvely puts forward his "incapacity for music" as a reason, perhaps the best, for not discussing the subject. It is not because they have dealt so scantily with the question that I have omitted references to Bain, Ladd, Stout, Ward, Wundt, and others, but because the reader will consult them in the first instance, and this applies as well to standard works on Anatomy and Physiology. Herbert Spencer's larger studies are so well known that they too come under this category, but I have noted some isolated articles of his to which the title of the volume containing them does not give a clue. It is not a little unfortunate that three of the most important works—those by Gurney, Dauriac and Lalo are not indexed, and some of their opinions, of the utmost value in a study of this kind, may be overlooked owing to this serious defect.

The reader must be warned that none of the books specified below discusses the subject from the dual point of view set forth in the preceding pages. All that has been possible here has been to give a list which may guide him in classifying the results of his own observation.

Apollo, Hymnus an: aus dem 3. Jahrhundert v. Chr. wieder aufgefunden 1893 in Delphi. Eingerichtet von A. Thierfelder. Leipzig: Breitkopf & Haertel, 1896.

Apollo, Hymn to: Composed about B.C. 378, transcribed by Théodore Reinach. London: Novello, Ewer & Co., not dated.

(Thierfelder's transcription begins at bar 30 of the above. The versions do not correspond throughout.)

BASTIAN, H. CHARLTON: *The Brain as an Organ of the Mind.* Third ed. London, 1885.

BATESON, W.: *Mendel's Principles of Heredity.* Cambridge, 1909.

BAZAILLAS, ALBERT: *Musique et Inconscience: Introduction à la Psychologie de l'Inconscient.* Paris, 1908.

BRACKENBURY, LAURA: *A Primer of Psychology.* Second ed. London, 1909.

BURNEY, CHARLES: *The Present State of Music in France and Italy: or, the Journal of a Tour through those Countries, undertaken to collect Materials for a General History of Music.* 2nd ed. London, 1773.

BURNEY, CHARLES: *The Present State of Music in Germany, the Netherlands, and United Provinces: or, The Journal of a Tour through those Countries, undertaken to collect Materials for a General History of Music.* 2 vols. 2nd ed. London, 1775.

BUTTEL-REEPEN, HUGO VON: *Man and his Forerunners.* Authorized translation by A. G. Thacker. London, 1913.

CHANTAVOINE, JEAN: *Musiciens et Poètes.* Paris, 1912.

COMBARIEU, JULES: *La Musique, ses Lois, son Evolution.* Paris, 1907.

COOMARASWAMY, ANANDA K.: *Essays in National Idealism.* Colombo, not dated.

(Contains chapters on "Indian Music," "Music and Education in India," and "Gramophones—and why not?")

DANION, L.: *La Musique et l'Oreille, Bases Rationnelles de la Musique. Le Faux Pas de l'Art Nouveau ou Musique dite de l'Avenir.* Paris, 1907.

DAURIAC, LIONEL: *Essai sur l'Esprit musical.* Paris, 1904.

(Valuable as a record of personal observation and independent in point of view. Not indexed.)

DECHÉLETTE, JOSEPH: *Manuel d'Archéologie préhistorique.* Paris, 1908-1913.

EGGER, VICTOR: *La Parole intérieure.* Second ed. Paris, 1904.

(Pages 73-74 refer to music.)

ELLIS, HAVELOCK: *A Study of British Genius.* London, 1904.

FERRIER, [SIR] DAVID, and TURNER, WILLIAM ALDREN: *An experimental Research upon cerebro-cortical afferent and efferent Tracts.* Trans. R. S. London, 1898.

FERRIER [SIR] DAVID: *The Functions of the Brain.* Second ed. London, 1886.

FORSYTH, CECIL: *Music and Nationalism, a Study of English Opera.* London, 1911.

GALTON, FRANCIS: *Hereditary Genius.* Second ed. London, 1892; First ed., 1869; re-issue, 1914.

GASPÉRINI, A. DE: *La nouvelle Allemagne musicale; Richard Wagner.* Paris, 1866.

GLASENAPP, CARL F.: *The Life of Richard Wagner.* Translated by Wm. Ashton Ellis. London, 1900.

GLYN, MARGARET H.: *The Rhythmic Conception of Music.* London, 1907.

GLYN, MARGARET H.: *Analysis of the Evolution of Musical Form.* London, 1909.

GURNEY, EDMUND: *The Power of Sound.* London, 1880.

HAMERTON, PHILIP GILBERT: *The Intellectual Life.* London, 1911. First ed., 1873.

HELMHOLTZ, HERMANN L. F.: *On the Sensations of Tone as a Physiological Basis for the Theory of Music.* Translated with additional Notes and Appendix by Alexander J. Ellis. Third ed. London, 1895.

HERVEY, ARTHUR: *Franz Liszt and his Music.* London, 1911.

HOWE, MAUD, and HALL, FLORENCE HOWE: *Laura Bridgman, Dr. Howe's famous Pupil and what he taught her.* Boston, U.S.A., 1903.

HURST, C. C.: *Mendel's Law of Heredity and its Application to Man. Trans. Leicester Lit. and Philosoph. Soc.* Vol. xii. Pt. 1. January, 1908.

HURST, C. C.: *Mendelian Heredity in Man. The Eugenics Review,* Vol. iv. April, 1912.

KELLER, HELEN: *The Story of my Life,* with her Letters (1887-1901) and a supplementary Account of her Education, including Passages from the Reports and Letters of her Teacher, Anne Mansfield Sullivan, by John Albert Macy. London, 1903.

KELVIN, LORD: *The Six Gateways of Knowledge.* Popular Lectures and Addresses, Vol. 1. London, 1891.

LAMB, CHARLES: *Sanity of true Genius.* Last Essays of Elia. London, 1903.

LALO, CHARLES: *Esquisse d'une Esthétique musicale scientifique.* Paris, 1908.

(A work showing immense research, and of first importance, but unfortunately not indexed.)

LAMY, F.: *Jean-François Le Sueur*, 1760-1837. Paris, 1912.

LAVOIX FILS, H.: *Histoire de l'Instrumentation depuis le Seizième Siècle jusqu'à nos Jours.* Paris, 1878.

LOEB, JACQUES: *Comparative Physiology of the Brain and Psychology.* London, 1901.

LOMBROSO, CESARE: *The Man of Genius.* London, 1891.

MACDONALD, PROF. J. S.: *Address to the Physiological Section* of the British Association. Portsmouth Meeting, 1911.

McEWEN, JOHN B.: *The Thought in Music—an Enquiry into the Principles of Musical Rhythm, Phrasing and Expression.* London, 1912.

McKENDRICK, JOHN GRAY, and SNODGRASS, WILLIAM: *The Physiology of the Senses.* London, 1893.

MENDEL, HERMANN: *Musicalisches Conversations-Lexikon*, 12 vols. Berlin, 1881-1883.

NEWMAN, ERNEST: *Gluck and the Opera, a Study in Musical History.* London, 1895.

NEWMAN, ERNEST: *A Study of Wagner.* London, 1899.

NEWMAN, ERNEST: *Musical Studies.* London, 1905.

NEWMAN, ERNEST: *Wagner as Man and Artist.* London, 1914.

NEWMARCH, ROSA: *Henry J. Wood.* Living Masters of Music. London, 1904.

(Contains a reference to the adoption of French pitch by the Queen's Hall Orchestra.)

NIECKS, FREDERICK: *Programme Music in the last four Centuries: a Contribution to the History of Musical Expression.* London, not dated.

NISBET, J. F.: *The Insanity of Genius and the general Inequality of human Faculty physiologically considered.* Fifth ed. London, not dated.

NORDAU, MAX: *Degeneration.* Fifth ed. London, 1895.

PEARSON, KARL: *The Grammar of Science.* Second ed. London, 1900.

PEREZ, BERNARD: *The First Three Years of Childhood.* Edited and translated by Alice M. Christie; with an *Introduction* by James Sully, M.A. London, 1885.

(Pages 265-270 deal with the child's music-sense.)

POINCARÉ, HENRI: *Science and Method.* Translated by Francis Maitland with a Preface by the Hon. Bertrand Russell, F.R.S. London [1914].

PUNNETT, R. C.: *Mendelism.* Fourth ed. London, 1912.

PUSCHMANN, TH.: *Richard Wagner, eine psychiatrische Studie.* Berlin, 1873.

RAYMOND, GEORGE LANSING: *Rhythm and Harmony in Poetry and Music, together with Music as a representative Art.* New York, 1895.

REID, GEORGE ARCHDALL O'BRIEN: *The Principles of Heredity.* London, 1905.

REID, GEORGE ARCHDALL O'BRIEN: *The Laws of Heredity.* London, 1910.

REINACH, SALOMON: *Répertoire de l'Art quaternaire.* Paris, 1913.

(Gives copies of prehistoric drawings, paintings and sculpture.)

RIBOT, THÉODULE ARMAND: *Psychologie de l'Attention.* Paris, 1889. Authorised English translation, Chicago, 1890.

RIBOT, THÉODULE ARMAND: *The Psychology of the Emotions.* London, 1897.

RIEMANN, HUGO: *Les Éléments de l'Esthétique musicale.* Paris, 1906.

ROLLAND, ROMAIN: *Musiciens d'aujourd'hui.* Second ed. Paris, 1908.

ROUSSEAU, J. J.: *Essai sur l'Origine des Langues, où il est parlé de la Mélodie, et de l'Imitation musicale.* Paris, 1817.

SAINT-SAËNS, CAMILLE: *Harmonie et Mélodie.* Paris, 1885.

(Referring to Eastern music, on p. 271, he observes, "Ce grand art de l'antiquité et de l'Orient n'est ni supérieur ni inférior au nôtre, d'un façon absolue : c'est un autre art.")

SCHURÉ, ÉDOUARD: *Le Drame musical.* Paris, 1875.

SHAW, GEORGE BERNARD: *The Sanity of Art: an Exposure of the current Nonsense about Artists being degenerate.* London, 1908.

(Contains the reply to Nordau's *Degeneration.*)

SPEARING, H. G.: *The Childhood of Art or the Ascent of Man.* London, 1912.

SPENCER, HERBERT: *Facts and Comments.* London, 1902.

(Contains "The Corruption of Music," "Feeling *versus* Intellect," "Purpose of Art," "The Origin of Music," "Developed Music," "Meyerbeer," "Some Musical Heresies.")

SPILLER, GUSTAV: *The Mind of Man.* London, 1902.

(Gives a summary of the views held by various authorities on points that are discussed, and contains a comprehensive bibliography.)

STANFORD, SIR CHARLES VILLIERS: *Musical Composition.* London, 1911.

STRANGWAYS, A. F. FOX: *The Music of Hindostan.* London, 1914.

STUMPF, CARL: *Tonpsychologie.* Leipzig, erster Band, 1883; zweiter Band, 1890.

SULLY, JAMES: *Sensation and Intuition: Studies in Psychology and Æsthetics.* London, 1874.

(Contains important articles on "The Basis of Musical Sensation," "Aspects of Beauty in Musical Form," and "The Nature and Limits of Musical Expression.")

SULLY, JAMES: *Studies of Childhood.* London, 1895.

(See also under Perez.)

THOMSON, J. ARTHUR: *Heredity.* London, 1908.

THOMSON, WILLIAM HANNA: *Brain and Personality, or the Physical Relations of the Brain to the Mind.* London, 1907.

TÜRCK, HERMANN: *The Man of Genius.* First English ed. Schwerin, I.M., 1914.

(Ch. x., p. 305, discusses and refutes Lombroso's Hypothesis of Insanity.)

VEBLEN, THORSTEIN B.: *The Theory of the Leisure Class.* New York, 1899.

Wagner, Richard to Minna, Letters to his first Wife. Translated, prefaced, etc., by William Ashton Ellis. London, 1909.

WAGNER, RICHARD: *My Life.* 2 vols. London, 1911.

WALLACE, WILLIAM: *The Scope of Programme Music. Proc. of the Musical Association.* London, 1899.

WALLACE, WILLIAM: *The Threshold of Music, an Inquiry into the Development of the Musical Sense.* London, 1908.

WEININGER, OTTO: *Sex and Character.* London, 1906.

(The following extracts are of interest: "The more gifted a man is, the more he has studied on his own account, and the more subjects he has made his own. . . . The theory of special genius, according to which, for instance, it is supposed that a musical 'genius' should be a fool at other subjects, confuses genius with talent. A musician, if truly great, is just as well able to be universal in his knowledge as a philosopher or poet. Such an one was Beethoven. On the other hand, a musician may be as limited in the sphere of his activity as any average man of science. . . . There are many kinds of talent, but only one kind of genius, and that is able to choose any kind of talent and master it" (p. 112). "Music is the nearest possible approach to the organization of a sensation. Nothing is more definite, characteristic, and impressive than a melody, nothing will more strongly resist obliteration. One remembers much longer what is sung than what is spoken, and the arias better than the recitatives" (p. 120).

ZIEHEN, THEODOR: *Introduction to Physiological Psychology.* Translated by C. C. Van Liew and Otto Beyer. London, 1892.

INDEX